Whether you are encountering French speakers in Europe or meeting them here,

whether you are facing a restaurant menu or a hotel desk clerk,

whether you are visiting a museum or stopping at a gas station,

whether you need directions or want to strike up a casual conversation,

whether you have to deal with a medical emergency or a mechanical breakdown,

whether you want to establish trust and good feelings in a business meeting or demonstrate warmth and courtesy in personal dealings,

this one book is your—

PASSPORT TO FRENCH

REVISED AND EXPANDED EDITION

REVISED AND EXPANDED EDITION
CHARLES BERLITZ
PASSPORT TO
FRENCH

A SIGNET BOOK

NEW AMERICAN LIBRARY

A DIVISION OF PENGUIN BOOKS USA INC., NEW YORK
PUBLISHED IN CANADA BY
PENGUIN BOOKS CANADA LIMITED, MARKHAM, ONTARIO

NAL BOOKS ARE AVAILABLE AT QUANTITY DISCOUNTS WHEN USED TO
PROMOTE PRODUCTS OR SERVICES. FOR INFORMATION PLEASE WRITE
TO PREMIUM MARKETING DIVISION, NEW AMERICAN LIBRARY,
1633 BROADWAY, NEW YORK, NEW YORK 10019.

Published by arrangement with Charles Berlitz

 SIGNET TRADEMARK REG. U.S. PAT. OFF. AND FOREIGN COUNTRIES
REGISTERED TRADEMARK–MARCA REGISTRADA
HECHO EN WINNIPEG, CANADA

SIGNET, SIGNET CLASSIC, MENTOR, ONYX, PLUME, MERIDIAN AND
NAL BOOKS are published by New American Library, a division of
Penguin Books USA Inc., 1633 Broadway, New York, New York 10019

First Signet Printing, April, 1974
First Printing (Revised and Expanded Edition), June, 1986

3 4 5 6 7 8 9 10 11

PRINTED IN CANADA

Contents

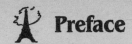 **Preface**

Is it possible to learn to speak French from a phrase book? If one means basic communication—the ability to speak, understand, and generally get along—the answer is yes—*if* you learn the right phrases. The secret of learning languages is to learn not only individual words, but also the phrases in which they are apt to occur on a frequency basis—as the French use them every day.

The purpose of this book is to provide instant communication in French. The phrases are short, geared to situations of daily life, and pinpointed for easy reference so that you can find the exact section you need at any moment.

There is even a chapter—"Words That Show You Are 'With It' "—that gives you the key words and phrases that French people use to add color to their conversation. In this way, instead of learning about "the umbrella of my aunt," you learn to use the right phrase at the right time, in the very way a French person would use it. And, so that French people will understand your accent, all you have to do is read the phonetic line under each French phrase *as if it were English.* Further practice and listening to French people speaking will improve your accent.

The use of this book is not limited to a trip to France, Canada, Belgium, Switzerland, or other French-speaking countries. French is spoken throughout the world, and, besides the pleasure and help you will get by speaking French on your travels, you will find it an additional pleasure to use the idiomatic French you will learn in this book in French restaurants and with French-speaking people you may meet anywhere.

Travelers using phrase books sometimes complain that when they ask a question or make a request to a native speaker of the language, they cannot understand the answer they get. This has been solved in *Passport to French* by an original and effective expedient. After the first few sections a special insert called "Point to the Answer" appears at the end of certain sections. You simply show this material to the person to whom you are speaking and let him or her point to the appropriate answer. This is an assured way of instant communication, and besides its evident usefulness, it will give you added confidence. Since you are communicating in this way in French with a French person, it will constantly improve your understanding of the language.

Young people studying French in a more conventional manner in school or college will find this book invaluable as an aid to their studies in that it brings modern colloquial French alive as a means of communication.

The use of this book will more than double your enjoyment of a trip abroad and also help you save money. Besides the economic factor, why visit a foreign country if you can't break the language barrier and communicate with the new and interesting people you meet? You might as well stay home and see the palaces and monuments of the country on color TV. Why be limited to one language when picking up another language can be so easy and enjoyable?

One can speak and understand current everyday French with comparatively few words and phrases—perhaps 1,500 to 1,800—which is less than the number given in the speaking dictionary at the end of this book. By using the same short constructions over and over in the various situations where they normally occur, you will acquire them without conscious effort. They will become a part of your own vocabulary and of your memory bank, and that is, after all, the only "secret" of learning a language.

How to Acquire an Instant French Accent

Every word or sentence in this book is presented in English, in French, and in easy-to-read phonetics to help you pronounce the French you see. Just pronounce the phonetics as if you were reading English, with the following exceptions:

1. We have expressed the French **u** in the phonetics as *ů*. To make this sound, pronounce "ee" with your lips rounded in a tight circle as if to whistle. For example, the well-known Rue de la Paix is pronounced *rů duh la pay*.

2. The French nasal sound of "n" is expressed by *n*, a signal to stop breathing and say it through your nose.

(English)	No.
(French)	Non.
(Phonetics)	*nohn.*

3. The soft French **j** is expressed by *zh* in the phonetics. This is pronounced like the "s" in "measure."

I travel a lot.
Je voyage beaucoup.
zhuh vwa-yahzh bo-koo.

French word linkage is expressed in the phonetics by attaching the "linking" letter to the next word, just as it sounds.

Where are they?
Où sont-ils?
oo sohn-teel?

French **a** is pronounced like the *a* in the English word *pa*. French **o** is pronounced like the *o* in the English word *so*. An additional piece of advice will enable you to sound even more like a true son or daughter of France: French syllables have nearly equal stress, but give a slight additional emphasis to the *last* syllable of every phrase.

> **Paris is my favorite city.**
> Paris est ma ville préférée.
> *pa-ree ay ma veel pray-fay-RAY.*

With this advice and the easy phonetic system we have devised, you will certainly be told:

> Vous avez un très bon accent!
> *voo za-vay un tray bohn nak-sahn!*

This means, "You have a very good accent!"

1. Greetings and Introductions

When addressing people, call them **Monsieur, Madame, Mademoiselle**—with or *without* the last name. Even when you say simply **Bonjour!** ("Good morning!" or "Good day!") it is more polite to add one of these forms of address.

Mr. or Sir
Monsieur
muss-yuh

Mrs. or Madam
Madame
ma-dahm

Miss
Mademoiselle
mahd-mwa-zell

Good morning (or)
  Good afternoon, sir.
Bonjour, Monsieur.
bohn-zhoor, muss-yuh.

Good evening, madam.
Bonsoir, Madame.
bohn-swahr, ma-dahm.

How are you?
Comment allez-vous?
ko-mahn tal-lay-voo?

Very well, thank you. And you?
Très bien, merci. Et vous?
tray b'yen, mair-see. ay voo?

Come in.
Entrez.
ahn-tray.

Sit down, please.
Asseyez-vous, s'il vous
  plaît.
ah-say-yay-voo, seel voo play.

I am Henry Marchant.
Je suis Henri Marchant.
*zhuh swee ahn-ree
  mahr-shahn.*

What is your name?
Quel est votre nom?
kel ay votr' nohn?

May I introduce . . .
Je vous présente . . .
zhuh voo pray-zahnt . . .

Delighted (to meet you).
Enchanté.
ahn-shahn-tay.

---

1. *Pronounce ů like ee with your lips in a tight circle.*
2. *zh is like the s in measure.*
3. *n means a nasal "n," pronounced through the nose.*

1

Are you American?
Êtes-vous américain?
  (f. américaine)
ett-voo za-may-ree-keñ?
  (za-may-ree-kane)

Yes, I am on a visit.
Oui, je suis en visite.
*wee, zhuh swee zahñ vee-
  zeet.*

Have a good stay in Paris.
Bon séjour à Paris.
bohñ say-zhoor ah pa-ree.

It's very kind (of you).
Très gentil.
tray zhahñ-tee'.

Good-bye.
Au revoir.
oh-ruh-vwahr.

Good night.
Bonne nuit.
bunn nwee.

See you soon.
A bientôt.
ah-b'yeñ-toh.

En passant (by the way): If you do not know whether a lady is married or not, address her as **Madame** rather than **Mademoiselle.** And to kiss a lady's hand is a gesture of respect toward a married woman.

2. Basic Expressions

Learn these by heart. You will use them every time you speak French to someone. If you memorize these expressions and the numbers in the next section, you will find that you can ask prices and directions and generally make your wishes known.

Yes	No	Perhaps	Please	Thank you
Oui	Non	Peut-être	S'il vous plaît	Merci
wee	*nohn*	*puh-tetr'*	*seel voo play*	*mair-see*

You are welcome.	Pardon	I am sorry.
De rien.	Pardon	Je regrette.
duh-r'yen.	*par-dohn*	*zhuh ruh-grett.*

It's all right.	here	over there	this	that
Ça va.	ici	là-bas	ceci	cela
sa va.	*ee-see*	*la-ba*	*suh-see*	*suh-la*

Do you speak English?	I speak French—a little.
Parlez-vous anglais?	Je parle français—un peu.
par-lay voo zahn-glay?	*zhuh parl frahn-say—un puh.*

Do you understand?	I understand.
Comprenez-vous?	Je comprends.
kohn-pruh-nay voo?	*zhuh kohn-prahn.*

I don't understand.	Very well.
Je ne comprends pas.	Très bien.
zhuh nuh kohn-prahn pa.	*tray b'yen.*

---

1. *Pronounce ǔ like ee* with your lips in a tight circle.
2. *zh* is like the *s* in measure.
3. *n* means a nasal "n," pronounced through the nose.

Speak slowly, please.
Parlez lentement, s'il vous plaît.
par-lay lahn-mahn, seel voo play.

Repeat, please.
Répétez, s'il vous plaît.
ray-pay-tay, seel voo play.

Write it down.
Écrivez cela.
ay-kree-vay suh-la.

Who is it?
Qui est-ce?
kee ess?

Come in.
Entrez.
ahn-tray.

Don't come in.
N'entrez pas.
nahn-tray pa.

Stop!
Arrêtez!
ahr-ray-tay!

Wait!
Attendez!
ah-tahn-day!

Let's go.
Allons.
ahl-lohn.

That's all.
C'est tout.
say too.

What is this?
Qu'est-ce que c'est?
kess kuh say?

Where is the telephone?
Où est le téléphone?
oo ay luh tay-lay-fohn?

Where are the rest rooms?
Où sont les lavabos?
oo sohn lay la-va-bo?

. . . for ladies.
. . . pour dames.
. . . poor dahm.

. . . for men.
. . . pour hommes.
. . . poor ohm.

Show me . . .
Montrez-moi . . .
*mon-tray
mwa . . .*

How much?
Combien?
kohn-b'yen?

It's too much.
C'est trop.
say tro.

Who?
Qui?
kee?

When?
Quand?
kahn?

How far?
A quelle distance?
ah kel dees-tahnss?

How much time?
Combien de temps?
kohn-b'yen duh tahn?

How?
Comment?
ko-mahn?

Like this.
Comme ça.
kom sa.

Not like that.
Pas comme ça.
pa kom sa.

There it is!
Voilà!
vwa-la!

---

1. *Pronounce* ů like *ee* with your lips in a tight circle.
2. *zh* is like the *s* in measure.
3. *n̈* means a nasal "n," pronounced through the nose.

3. Numbers

The numbers are important not only for asking prices (and perhaps to bargain) but for phone numbers, addresses, and telling time. Learn the first twenty by heart and then from 20 to 100 by tens, and *voilà!* You have them!

1	**2**	**3**	**4**	**5**
un	deux	trois	quatre	cinq
un	*duh*	*trwa*	*katr'*	*senk*

6	**7**	**8**	**9**	**10**
six	sept	huit	neuf	dix
seess	*set*	*weet*	*nuff*	*deess*

11	**12**	**13**	**14**
onze	douze	treize	quatorze
ohnz	*dooz*	*trayz*	*ka-torz*

15	**16**	**17**	**18**
quinze	seize	dix-sept	dix-huit
kenz	*sayz*	*dee-set*	*dees-weet*

19	**20**	**21**
dix-neuf	vingt	vingt et un
dees-nuff	*ven*	*vent-ay-un*

22	**25**	**30**
vingt-deux	vingt-cinq	trente
vent-duh	*vent-senk*	*trahnt*

40	**50**	**60**
quarante	cinquante	soixante
ka-rahnt	*senk-ahnt*	*swa-sahnt*

---

1. *Pronounce* ǔ like *ee* with your lips in a tight circle.
2. *zh* is like the *s* in measure.
3. *n* means a nasal "n," pronounced through the nose.

70 (60 and 10)
soixante-dix
swa-sahnt-deess

71 (60 and 11)
soixante et onze
*swa-sahnt ay
ohnz*

80 (4 × 20)
quatre-vingts
katr'-ven

81 (4 × 20 + 1)
quatre-vingt-un
katr'-vent-un

90 (4 × 20 + 10)
quatre-vingt-dix
katr'-vent-deess

91 (4 × 20 + 11)
quatre-vingt-onze
katr'-vent-ohnz

100
cent
sahn

110
cent dix
sahn deess

200
deux cents
duh sahn

300
trois cents
trwa sahn

a half
un demi
un duh-mee

and a half
et demi (-e)
ay duh-mee

1000
mille
meel

100,000
cent mille
sahn meel

1,000,000
un million
un meel-yohn

first
premier (m), première (f)
pruhm-yay, pruhm-yair

second
deuxième
duhz-yem

third
troisième
trwahz-yem

last
dernier (m), dernière (f)
dairn-yay, dairn-yair

How much? (or) How many?
Combien?
kohn-b'yen?

What number?
Quel numéro?
kel nů-may-ro?

En passant: Seventy is formed by the combination "sixty-ten" (soixante-dix), and 71, 72, 73, etc., by combining 60 with 11, 12, 13, and so on, right through the teens: **soixante et onze, soixante douze, soixante treize,** etc. The same thing happens with 80, which is literally "four twenties"—**quatre-**

vingts, which becomes, for 91, 92, etc., **quatre-vingt-onze, quatre-vingt-douze,** etc.

All French nouns are either masculine or feminine, and most adjectives, such as *first* and *last,* have a masculine and feminine form. (See above.)

---

1. *Pronounce* ů like *ee* with your lips in a tight circle.
2. *zh* is like the *s* in measure.
3. *n* means a nasal "n," pronounced through the nose.

🗼 4. Arrival

Besides exchanging some words with airport officials, one of the most important things you will want to do on arrival in France is to find your way around. For this reason we offer you here some basic "asking your way" questions and answers and call your attention to the "Point to the Answer" sections which the people to whom you speak can use to *point out* answers to make it easier for you to understand.

Your passport, please.
Votre passeport, s'il vous plaît.
votr' pass-por, seel voo play.

I am on a visit.
Je suis de passage.
zhuh swee duh pa-sahzh.

For three weeks.
Pour trois semaines.
poor trwa suh-men.

I am on a business trip.
Je suis en voyage d'affaires.
zhuh swee zahn vwa-yahzh daf-fair.

Where are the bags?
Où sont les valises?
oo sohn lay va-leez?

For flight 105.
Pour le vol cent cinq.
poor luh vohl sahn sank.

Where is the customs?
Où est la douane?
oo ay la dwahn?

Here are my bags.
Voilà mes valises.
vwa-la may va-leez.

Nothing to declare.
Rien à déclarer.
r'yen ah day-kla-ray.

All right. Go on.
C'est bien. Passez.
say b'yen. pa-say.

---

1. *Pronounce* ü like *ee* with your lips in a tight circle.
2. *zh* is like the *s* in measure.
3. *n* means a nasal "n," pronounced through the nose.

Where is the bus to the city?
Où est l'autobus pour la ville?
oo ay lo-toh-bùss poor la veel?

Where are the taxis?
Où sont les taxis?
oo sohn lay tahk-see?

Where is there a telephone?
Où y a-t-il un téléphone?
oo ee-ya-teel un tay-lay-fohn?

Where are the rest rooms?
Où sont les toilettes?
oo sohn lay twa-lett?

Porter!
Porteur!
por-turr!

Please take these bags to a taxi.
S'il vous plaît; portez ces valises à un taxi.
Seel voo play; por-tay say va-leez ah un tahk-see.

I'll carry this one myself.
Je porte celle-ci moi-même.
zhuh port sell-see mwa-mem.

How much do I owe you?
Combien je vous dois?
kohn-b'yen zhuh voo dwa?

Taxi, are you free?
Taxi, êtes-vous libre?
tahk-see, ett-voo leebr'?

To the Hotel Crillon, please.
A l'Hôtel Crillon, s'il vous plaît.
ah lo-tel kree-yohn, seel voo play.

To the Hotel de Paris.
A l'Hôtel de Paris.
ah lo-tel duh pa-ree.

How much is it?
C'est combien?
say kohn-b'yen?

Where is . . .
Où est . . .
oo ay . . .

. . . the Louvre?
. . . le Louvre?
. . . luh loovr'?

. . . the Madeleine?
. . . la Madeleine?
. . . la mahd-lain?

. . . Notre Dame?
. . . Notre Dame?
. . . nohtr' dàhm?

. . . the Latin Quarter?
. . . le quartier latin?
. . . luh kar-t'yeh la-ten?

. . . Monmartre?
. . . Montmartre?
. . . *mohn-mahtr'?*

. . . **the address written here?**
. . . L'adresse écrite ici?
. . . *la-dress eh-kreet ee-see?*

. . . **the bus stop?**
. . . l'arrêt des omnibus?
. . . *la-reh days oh-toh-bůss?*

. . . **the taxi stand?**
. . . la station des taxis?
. . . *la sta-s'yohn day tahk-see?*

. . . **the subway entrance?**
. . . la bouche du métro?
. . . *la boosh du may-tro?*

Where can one find . . .
Où peut-on trouver . . .
oo puh-tohn troo-vay . . .

. . . **a good restaurant?**
. . . un bon restaurant?
. . . *un bohn res-toh-rahn?*

. . . **a drugstore?**
. . . une pharmacie?
. . . *ůne far-ma-see?*

. . . **a barbershop?**
. . . un coiffeur?
. . . *un kwa-fur?*

. . . **the post office?**
. . . le bureau de poste?
. . . *luh bů-ro duh post?*

. . . **a hospital?**
. . . un hôpital?
. . . *un o-pee-tahl?*

. . . **the American consulate?**
. . . le consulat américain?
. . . *luh kohn-sů-la ah-may-ree-ken?*

British?
britannique?
bree-ta-neek?

Canadian?
canadien?
ka-nahd-yen?

Thank you very much.
Merci bien.
mair-see b'yen.

You are very kind.
Vous êtes très aimable.
voo zett trays aim-ahbl'.

---

1. *Pronounce ů like ee* with your lips in a tight circle.
2. *zh* is like the *s* in measure.
3. *n* means a nasal "n," pronounced through the nose.

POINT TO THE ANSWER

To make sure that you understand the answer to a question you have asked, show the following section to a French person so that he or she can select the answer. The sentence in French after the arrow asks the other person to point out the answer.

 Veuillez indiquer ci-dessous la réponse à ma question. Merci.

Suivez cette rue jusq'à la rue _____ .
Follow this street until _____ Street.

À droite.   **A gauche.**   **Au coin.**
To the right.   To the left.   On the corner.

Encore trois rues.
Three streets more.

Tournez à gauche en arrivant à _____ .
Turn left when you get to _____ .

Suivez l'Avenue de l'Opéra.
Follow the Avenue of the Opera.

C'est loin?   **Non.**   **C'est tout près.**
Is it far?   No.   It's quite near.

C'est loin.   **Prenez l'autobus.**
It's far.   Take the bus.

là-bas, au coin.
over there, on the corner.

Descendez à _____ .
Get off at _____ .

Prenez le métro.
Take the subway.

En passant: When you speak to a stranger, don't forget to say **Pardon, Monsieur** (or **Madame**) before you ask a question. If you talk to a policeman, you can call him **Monsieur** too.

French streets have white-on-blue signs on the buildings at each corner, making it easy to find out where you are.

To make sure you understand people's answers, you can show them the "Point to the Answer" sections in Chapters 5, 8, 10, 11, 12, and 16.

---

1. _Pronounce ǔ like ee_ with your lips in a tight circle.
2. _zh_ is like the _s_ in measure.
3. _n_ means a nasal "n," pronounced through the nose.

5. Hotel—Laundry—Dry Cleaning

Although the staffs of the larger hotels have some training in English, you will find that the use of French makes for better understanding and better relations, especially with the service personnel. Besides, it is fun, and you should practice French at every opportunity. We have included laundry and dry cleaning in this section, as these are subjects about which you have to make yourself understood in speaking to the chambermaid or valet in the hotel.

Can you recommend a good hotel?
Pouvez-vous recommander un bon hôtel?
poo-vay voo ruh-ko-mahn-day un bohn notel?

. . . a guest house?
. . . une pension?
. . . une pahns-yohn?

. . . in the center of town.
. . . dans le centre de la ville.
dahn luh sahntr' duh la veel.

. . . not too expensive.
. . . pas trop cher.
. . . pa tro shair.

I have a reservation.
J'ai une réservation.
zhay une ray-zair-vahs-yohn.

My name is Richard Dupont.
Je m'appelle Richard Dupont.
zhuh ma-pell ree-shahr dü-pohn.

Have you a room?
Avez-vous une chambre?
ah-vay voo zune shahnbr'?

I would like a room . . .
Je voudrais une chambre . . .
zhuh voo-dray zune shahnbr' . . .

---

1. *Pronounce ü* like *ee* with your lips in a tight circle.
2. *zh* is like the *s* in measure.
3. *n* means a nasal ''n,'' pronounced through the nose.

. . . **for one person.**
. . . pour une personne.
. . . *poor ůne pair-sonn.*

. . . **for two people.**
. . . pour deux personnes.
. . . *poor duh pair-sonn.*

. . . **with two beds.**
. . . à deux lits.
. . . *ah duh lee.*

. . . **with a bathroom.**
. . . avec salle de bain.
. . . *ah-vek sahl duh ben.*

. . . **hot water.**
. . . de l'eau chaude.
. . . *duh lo shohd.*

. . . **air-conditioned.**
. . . climatisée.
. . . *klee-ma-tee-zay.*

. . . **with a balcony.**
. . . avec un balcon.
. . . *ah-vek un bahl-kohn.*

. . . **with television.**
. . . avec la télévision.
. . . *ah-vek la tay-lay-veez-yohn.*

How does this work?
Comment ceci marche-t-il?
ko-mahn suh-see marsh-teel?

How much is it?   . . . **per day?**   . . . **per week?**
C'est combien?   . . . par jour?   . . . par semaine?
say kohn-b'yen   . . . *par zhoor?*   . . . *par suh-men?*

Are the meals included?
Est-ce que les repas sont compris?
ess kuh lay ruh-pa sohn kohn-pree?

Is breakfast included?
Est-ce que le petit déjeuner est compris?
ess kuh luh puh-tee day-zhuh-nay ay kohn-pree?

I should like to see the room.
Je voudrais voir la chambre.
zhuh voo-dray vwar la shahnbr'.

Where is the toilet?   . . . **the shower?**
Où est la toilette?   . . . la douche?
oo ay la twa-let?   . . . *la doosh?*

I want another room.   . . . **higher up.**
Je veux une autre chambre.   . . . plus haut.
zhuh vuh zůne otr' shahnbr'.   . . . *plů oh.*

. . . **better.**   . . . **larger.**   . . . **smaller.**
. . . meilleure.   . . . plus grande.   . . . plus petite.
. . . *may-yurr.*   . . . *plů grahnd.*   . . . *plů puh-teet.*

I'll take this room.   **I'll stay for _____ days.**
Je prends cette chambre.   Je resterai _____ jours.
zhuh prahn set shahnbr'.   *zhuh ress-tuh-ray _____ zhoor.*

What time is lunch served?   **What time is dinner served?**
A quelle heure sert-on le   A quelle heure sert-on le
  déjeuner?   dîner?
ah kel err sair-tohn luh   *ah kel err sair-tohn luh*
  day-zhuh-nay?   *dee-nay?*

I want to be called at 8 o'clock.
Je voudrais qu'on m'appelle à huit heures.
zhuh voo-dray kohn ma-pel ah weet err.

Bring breakfast to number _____ .
Faites monter le petit déjeuner au numéro _____ .
fett mohn-tay luh puh-tee day-zhuh-nay
  oh nů-may-ro _____ .

A continental breakfast (coffee, hot milk, rolls, butter, jam).
Un café complet.
un ka-fay kohn-play.

---

1. *Pronounce ů* like *ee* with your lips in a tight circle.
2. *zh* is like the *s* in measure.
3. *n* means a nasal "n," pronounced through the nose.

For a choice of breakfast foods, see page 31.

I would like . . .   **. . . some ice.**
Je voudrais . . .   . . . de la glace.
zhuh voo-dray . . .   *. . . duh la glahss.*

. . . a bottle of mineral water.
. . . une bouteille d'eau minérale.
. . . ûne boo-tay doh mee-nay-rahl.

Will you send these letters?   **Will you put stamps on**
Voulez-vous expédier ces   **them?**
  lettres?   Voulez-vous les timbrer?
voo-lay-voo ex-paid-yay   *voo-lay-voo lay taꞑ-bray?*
  say lettr'?

The key, please.   **Is there any mail for me?**
La clé, s'il vous plaît.   Y a-t-il du courrier pour moi?
la klay, seel yoo play.   *ee ya teel du koor-yay poor mwa?*

Send my mail to this address.
Faites suivre mon courrier à cette adresse.
fett sweevr' mohꞑ koor-yay ah set ah-dress.

I want to talk with the manager.
Je veux parler avec le directeur.
zhuh vuh par-lay ah-vek luh dee-rek-turr.

I need an interpreter.
J'ai besoin d'un interprète.
zhay buh-zweꞑ duꞑ neꞑ-tair-pret.

Are you the chambermaid?
Etes-vous la femme de chambre?
et-voo la fahm duh shahꞑbr'?

Will you change the sheets?   **I need . . .**
Voulez-vous changer les draps?   J'ai besoin . . .
voo-lay-voo shahꞑ-zhay lay drah? *zhay buh-zweꞑ . . .*

. . . a blanket.
. . . d'une couverture.
. . . *d'une koo-vair-tŭr.*

. . . a pillow.
. . . d'un oreiller.
. . . *dun noh-ray-yay.*

. . . a towel.
. . . d'une serviette.
. . . *d'une sair-v'yet.*

. . . some soap.
. . . de savon.
. . . *duh sa-vohn.*

. . . some toilet paper.
. . . de papier hygiénique.
. . . *duh pap-yay eezh-yay-neek.*

This is to be cleaned.
Ceci est à nettoyer.
suh-see ay ta net-twa-yay.

This is to be pressed.
Ceci est à repasser.
suh-see ay ta ruh-pa-say.

This is to be repaired.
Ceci est à réparer.
suh-see ay ta ray-pa-ray.

This is to be washed.
Ceci est à laver.
suh-see ay ta la-vay.

For this evening?
Pour ce soir?
poor suh swahr?

. . . tomorrow?
. . . demain?
. . . *duh-men?*

. . . tomorrow afternoon?
. . . demain après-midi?
. . . *duh-men
ah-pray-mee-dee?*

. . . tomorrow evening?
. . . demain soir?
. . . *duh-men swahr?*

When?
Quand?
kahn?

Without fail?
Sans faute?
sahn foht?

Be very careful with this.
Attention à ceci.
ah-tahns-yohn ah suh-see.

---

1. *Pronounce ŭ like ee* with your lips in a tight circle.
2. *zh* is like the *s* in measure.
3. *n* means a nasal "n," pronounced through the nose.

Are my clothes ready?
Mes vêtements sont-ils prêts?
may vet-mahn sohn-teel pray?

Prepare my bill, please.
Préparez la note, s'il vous plaît.
pray-pa-ray la noht, seel voo play.

When is checkout time?
A quelle heure faut-il quitter la chambre?
A kell err fo-teel kee-tay la shahnbr'?

I'm leaving tomorrow morning.
Je pars demain matin.
zhuh par duh-men ma-ten.

Will you call me at 7 o'clock?   **It's important.**
Voulez-vous m'appeler à sept heures?   C'est important.
voo-lay-voo map-lay ah set err?   *say ten-por-*
                                            tahn.

En passant: Hotel floors are generally counted starting
above the ground floor—**rez de chaussée**—so that the second
floor is called the first, the third is the second, etc.
   Tips are included in the bill, but when something is
brought to your room, a small tip is seldom refused.

POINT TO THE ANSWER

To make sure that you understand the answer to your question, show the following section to the person to whom you
are speaking so he or she can select the answer. The sentence in French after the arrow asks him or her to point to
the answer.

>
> *Veuillez indiquer ci-dessous la réponse à ma*
> *question. Merci.*

Aujourd'hui.	**Cet après-midi.**	**Ce soir.**
Today.	This afternoon.	This evening.

Demain.	**De bonne heure.**	**Tard.**
Tomorrow.	Early.	Late.

Avant une heure.   **C'est possible.**
Before one o'clock.   It is possible.

Ce n'est pas possible.
It is not possible.

Avant deux (trois, quatre, cinq) heures.
Before two (three, four, five) o'clock.

A cinq (six, sept, huit, neuf, dix, onze, douze) heures.
At five (six, seven, eight, nine, ten, eleven, twelve)
   o'clock.

lundi	**mardi**	**mercredi**
Monday	Tuesday	Wednesday

jeudi	**vendredi**	**samedi**	**dimanche**
Thursday	Friday	Saturday	Sunday

---

1. *Pronounce* ǔ *like* ee *with your lips in a tight circle.*
2. *zh* is like the *s* in measure.
3. *n* means a nasal "n," pronounced through the nose.

6. Time: Hours—Days—Months

In the hotel section you noted that when making an appointment at a certain hour you simply put *à* in front of the number, and then the word for "hour." "At nine o'clock" is **à neuf heures**. The following section shows you how to tell time in greater detail, including dates. You can make all sorts of arrangements with people by indicating the hour, the day, the date, and adding the phrase **C'est entendu?** "It is agreed?"

What time is it?
Quelle heure est-il?
kell err ay-teel?

It is one o'clock.
Il est une heure.
eel ay tůne err.

It is six o'clock.
Il est six heures.
eel ay see zerr.

half past . . .
. . . et demie
. . . *ay duh-mee*

a quarter past . . .
. . . et quart
. . . *ay kar*

a quarter to . . .
. . . moins le quart
. . . *mwen luh kar*

ten minutes past . . .
. . . dix
. . . *deess*

ten minutes to . . .
. . . moins dix
. . . *mwen deess*

at nine o'clock
à neuf heures
ah nuhf err

at exactly seven o'clock
à sept heures précises
ah set err prayseez

---

1. *Pronounce ů like ee with your lips in a tight circle.*
2. *zh is like the s in measure.*
3. *n means a nasal "n," pronounced through the nose.*

25

the morning	noon	the afternoon
le matin	midi	l'après-midi
luh ma-ten	*mee-dee*	*la-pray-mee-dee*

the evening	the night	midnight
le soir	la nuit	minuit
luh swahr	*la nwee*	*mee-nwee*

today	tomorrow	yesterday
aujourd'hui	demain	hier
oh-zhoor-dwee	*duh-men*	*ee-air*

this evening	tomorrow evening	yesterday evening
ce soir	demain soir	hier soir
suh swahr	*duh-men swahr*	*ee-air swahr*

this week	last week	next week
cette semaine	la semaine	la semaine
set suh-men	dernière	prochaine
	la suh-men	*la suh-men*
	dairn-yair	*pro-shen*

two weeks ago	this month	next month
il y a deux	ce mois-ci	le mois prochain
semaines	*suh mwa-see*	*luh mwa pro-shen*
eel ee ya duh		
suh-men		

several months ago	this year
il y a quelques mois	cette année
eel ee ya kel-kuh mwa	*set ah-nay*

last year	next year
l'année dernière	l'année prochaine
la-nay dairn-yair	*la-nay pro-shen*

1986
mille neuf cent quatre-vingt-six
meel nuhf sahn katr'-ven-seess

Monday
lundi
lun-dee

Tuesday
mardi
mar-dee

Wednesday
mercredi
mair-kruh-dee

Thursday
jeudi
zhuh-dee

Friday
vendredi
vahn-druh-dee

Saturday
samedi
sam-dee

Sunday
dimanche
dee-mahnsh

next Monday
lundi prochain
lun-dee pro-shen

last Tuesday
mardi dernier
*mar-dee
   dairn-yay*

on Fridays
le vendredi
*luh vahn-druh-
   dee*

January
janvier
zhan-v'yay

February
février
fay-vree-ay

March
mars
marss

April
avril
ah-vreel

May
mai
may

June
juin
zhwen

July
juillet
zhwee-yay

August
août
oo

September
septembre
sep-tahnbr'

October
octobre
ok-tobr'

November
novembre
no-vahnbr'

December
décembre
day-sahnbr'

---

1. *Pronounce ů* like *ee* with your lips in a tight circle.
2. *zh* is like the *s* in measure.
3. *n* means a nasal "n," pronounced through the nose.

On what date?
À quelle date?
ah kel daht?

March 1st
Le premier mars
luh pruhm-yay marss

March 2nd, 3rd, 4th, etc.
le deux mars, le trois, le quatre
luh duh marss, luh trwa, luh katr'

The 25th of December
Le 25 décembre
luh vent-senk day-sahnbr'

Merry Christmas!
Joyeux Noël!
zhwa-yuh no-ell!

The first of January
Le premier janvier
luh pruhm-yay zhahn-v'yay

Happy New Year!
Bonne Année!
bunn ah-nay!

Happy Birthday!
Bonne Fête!
bunn fett!

Congratulations!
Félicitations!
fay-lee-see-ta-s'yohn!

The 14th of July
  (Bastille Day)
Le quatorze juillet
luh ka-torz zhwee-yay

Long live France!
Vive la France!
veev la frahnss!

En passant: The last phrase of this section refers to Bastille Day—**le Jour de la Bastille.** Another occasion when everyone stops work takes place during August, when most people take an annual vacation. Shops bear the sign **Fermeture Annuelle** (annual closing).

7. French Money

This short section contains necessary vocabulary for changing money. **A propos** (in this regard) you will find that the French bills for 100, 200, and 500 francs are so artistic that one almost regrets having to spend them.

Where can one change money?
Où peut-on changer de l'argent?
oo puh tohn shahn-zhay duh lar-zhahn?

Can I change dollars here?
Puis-je changer des dollars ici?
pweezh shahn-zhay day doh-lar ee-see?

Where is a bank?
Où y a-t-il une banque?
oo ee-ya-teel ůne bahnk?

What time does the bank open?
A quelle heure ouvre la banque?
ah kel err oovr' la bahnk?

What time does it close?
A quelle heure ferme-t-elle?
ah kel err fairm-tell?

What's the dollar rate?
Quel est le cours du dollar?
kel ay luh coor dů doh-lar?

It's ten francs twenty to a dollar.
C'est dix francs vingt pour un dollar.
Say dee frahn ven poor un dol-lar.

I would like to change $50.
Je voudrais changer cinquante dollars.
zhuh voo-dray shahn-zhay sen-kahnt doh-lar.

---

1. *Pronounce ů like ee* with your lips in a tight circle.
2. *zh* is like the *s* in measure.
3. *n* means a nasal "n," pronounced through the nose.

Do you accept travelers' checks?
Acceptez-vous des chèques de
  voyage?
*ahk-sep-tay-voo day shek duh
  vwa-yahzh?*

Certainly.
Certainement.
sair-ten-mahn.

No, not here.
Non, pas ici.
nohn, pa zee-see.

I am sorry.
Je regrette.
zhuh ruh-grett.

Will you accept a check?
Acceptez-vous un chèque?
ahk-sep-tay-vooz un shek?

Have you any identification?
Avez-vous des papiers
  d'identité?
*ah-vay-voo day pap-yay
  dee-dahn-tee-tay?*

Yes, here is my passport.
Oui, voilà mon passeport.
wee, vwa-la mohn pass-por.

Give me twenty 100-franc notes.
Donnez-moi vingt billets de cent francs.
don-nay-mwa ven bee-yay duh sahn frahn.

I need some small change.
J'ai besoin de la petite monnaie.
zhay buh-zwen duh la puh-teet mo-nay.

8. Basic Foods

The foods and drinks mentioned in this section will enable you to be well fed, and in France that is very well indeed! The section that follows this will deal with special French dishes—representative of the **cuisine** ("style of cooking" or "kitchen") that is one of the many outstanding products of French culture.

breakfast	**orange juice**	**a grapefruit**
le petit déjeuner	du jus d'orange	un pample-
luh puh-tee	*dů zhů do-rahɴzh*	mousse
day-zhuh-nay		*uɴ pahɴ-pluh-*
		mooss

a continental breakfast (coffee, rolls, butter, and jam)
un café complet
uɴ ka-fay kohɴ-play

soft-boiled eggs	**some toast**	**croissants**
des oeufs à la coque	des toasts	croissants
day zuh ah la kok	*day toast*	*krwa-sahɴ*

fried eggs	**with bacon**	**with ham**
des oeufs sur le plat	au bacon	au jambon
day zuh sůr luh pla	*oh ba-kohɴ*	*oh zhahɴ-bohɴ*

an omelet	**scrambled eggs**
une omelette	des oeufs brouillés
ůne om-let	*day zuh broo-yay*

coffee with hot milk	**cocoa**	**tea**
du café au lait	du chocolat	du thé
dů ka-fay oh lay	*dů sho-ko-la*	*dů tay*

---

1. *Pronounce* ů *like* ee *with your lips in a tight circle.*
2. *zh is like the s in measure.*
3. *ɴ means a nasal "n," pronounced through the nose.*

lunch
le déjeuner
luh day-zhuh-nay

dinner
le dîner
luh dee-nay

Do you know a good restaurant?
Connaissez-vous un bon restaurant?
ko-nay-say-voo un bohn ress-toh-rahn?

A table for three.
Une table pour trois.
ûne tabl' poor trwa.

This way, please.
Par ici, s'il vous plaît.
par ee-see, seel voo play.

The menu, please.
La carte, s'il vous plaît.
la kart, seel voo play.

What's good?
Qu'est-ce qu'il y a de bon?
kess keel ya duh bohn?

What do you recommend?
Qu'est-ce que vous recommandez?
kess-kuh voo ruh-ko-mahn-day?

What is it?
Qu'est-ce que c'est?
kess-kuh say?

Good.
Bon.
bohn.

I'll take it.
Je le prends.
zhuh luh prahn.

First a cocktail.
D'abord un cocktail.
da-bor un kok-tail.

Then some appetizers.
Ensuite des hors d'oeuvres.
ahn-sweet day or duhvr'.

soup
du potage
dû po-tazh

fish
du poisson
dû pwa-sohn

oysters
des huitres
day zweetr'

shrimp
des crevettes
day kruh-vet

lobster
du homard
dû oh-mar

chicken	**duck**	**goose**
du poulet	du canard	de l'oie
dů poo-lay	*dů ka-nahr*	*duh lwah*

lamb chops	**roast leg of lamb**
des cotelettes d'agneau	du gigot d'agneau
day kohn-let da-n'yo	*dů zhee-go da-n'yo*

veal	**pork**	**ham**
du veau	du porc	du jambon
dů vo	*dů por*	*dů zhahn-bohn*

hamburger	**a steak**	**roast beef**
du steak haché	un steak	du rosbif
dů steak ah-shay	*un steak*	*dů rohz-beef*

well done	**medium**	**rare**	**very rare**
bien cuit	à point	saignant	bleu
b'yen kwee	*ah pwen*	*sen-yahn*	*bluh*

roasted	**broiled**	**fried**	**boiled**
rôti	grillé	frit	bouilli
ro-tee	*gree-yay*	*free*	*boo-yee*

vegetables	**potatoes**	**fried potatoes or French fries**
des légumes	des pommes de terre	des pommes frites
day lay-gůme	*day pom duh tair*	*day pom freet*

rice	**noodles**	**green beans**
du ris	des nouilles	des haricots verts
dů ree	*day nwee*	*day ar-ree-ko vair*

---

1. *Pronounce* ů *like* ee *with your lips in a tight circle.*
2. *zh is like the s in measure.*
3. *n means a nasal "n," pronounced through the nose.*

peas
des petits pois
day puh-tee pwa

carrots
des carottes
day ka-rot

spinach
des épinards
day zay-pee-nar

cabbage
des choux
day shoo

mushrooms
des champignons
day shahn-peen-yohn

celery
du céleri
dŭ sail-ree

asparagus
des asperges
day zas-pairzh

onions
des oignons
day zo-n'yohn

oil
de l'huile
duh lweel

vinegar
du vinaigre
dŭ vee-naigr'

salt
du sel
dŭ sel

lettuce
de la laitue
duh la lay-tŭ

tomatoes
des tomates
day to-maht

a salad
une salade
ŭne sa-lahd

pepper
du poivre
dŭ pwavr'

mustard
de la moutarde
duh la moo-tard

with garlic
avec de l'ail
ah-vek duh l'eye

without garlic
sans ail
sahnz eye

bread
du pain
dŭ pan

butter
du beurre
dŭ berr

What wine do you recommend?
Quel vin recommandez-vous?
kel ven ruh-koh-mahn-day-voo?

white wine
du vin blanc
dŭ van blahn

red wine
du vin rouge
dŭ van roozh

beer
de la bière
duh la b'yair

champagne
du champagne
dŭ shahn-pine

To your health!
A votre santé!
ah votr' sahn-tay!

fruits
des fruits
day frwee

grapes
des raisins
day ray-zen

peaches
des pêches
day pesh

oranges
des oranges
day zo-rahnzh

plums
des prunes
day prŭn

pears
des poires
day pwar

apples
des pommes
day pohm

bananas
des bananes
day ba-nahn

a dessert
un dessert
un day-sair

pastry
de la patisserie
duh la pa-teess-ree

cake
du gateau
dŭ ga-toh

cheese
du fromage
dŭ fro-mazh

ice cream
une glace
ŭne glahss

coffee
du café
dŭ ka-fay

demi-tasse
du café noir
dŭ ka-fay nwar

expresso
café filtre
ka-fay feeltr'

tea with lemon
du thé au citron
dŭ tay oh see-trohn

hot chocolate
du chocolat
dŭ sho-ko-la

More, please.
Encore, s'il vous plaît.
ahn-kor, seel voo play.

That's enough, thank you.
C'est assez, merci.
say ta-say, mair-see.

---

1. *Pronounce ŭ* like *ee* with your lips in a tight circle.
2. *zh* is like the *s* in measure.
3. *n* means a nasal "n," pronounced through the nose.

Waiter!	**Waitress!**
Garçon!	Mademoiselle!
Gar-sohn!	*mahd-mwa-zell!*

The check, please.	**Is the tip included?**
L'addition, s'il vous plaît.	Service compris?
la-deess-yohn, seel voo play.	*sair-veess kohn-pree?*

I think there is an error in the bill.
Je crois qu'il y a une erreur dans l'addition.
zhuh krwa keel ee ya ûne air-ruhr dahn la-deess-yohn.

Oh no, sir, look here.
Oh non, monsieur, regardez.
oh nohn, muss-yuh, ruh-gar-day.

It's true.	**It's okay.**
C'est vrai.	Ça va.
say vray.	*sa va.*

Here.	**Thank you, sir.**	**Good-bye.**
Voilà.	Merci, monsieur.	Au revoir.
vwa-la.	*mair-see, muss-yuh.*	*oh ruh-vwahr.*

En passant: The reason that we have prefaced foodstuffs with **du, de la, de l'** and **des** (all variants of "some" according to the gender or number of the word) is that in French you cannot say the item by itself. Wine, for example, must always be "the wine"—**le vin**—or "some wine"—**du vin**.

POINT TO THE ANSWER

When you are at a restaurant and you wish to make sure that you understand the menu, show the following section to the waiter so that he or she can select the answer. The sentence in French after the arrow asks him to point to the answer.

Veuillez indiquer ci-dessous la réponse à ma question. Merci.

C'est la spécialité de la maison.
It's the specialty of the house.

Ça vient tout de suite.
It's ready.

Ça prendra un quart d'heure.
It takes a quarter of an hour.

Nous n'en avons pas aujourd'hui.
We don't have it today.

C'est le plat du vendredi.
That is the Friday special.

C'est du poulet, du porc, de l'agneau, du veau, du boeuf, du steak, du lapin, du poisson, des crustacés, des escargots.
It is chicken, pork, lamb, veal, beef, steak, rabbit, fish, seafood, snails.

. . . avec des légumes.   **. . . avec une sauce.**
. . . with vegetables.   . . . with a sauce.

. . . garni.
. . . with trimmings.

---

1. *Pronounce* ů̊ *like* ee *with your lips in a tight circle.*
2. *zh is like the* s *in measure.*
3. *n̄ means a nasal "n," pronounced through the nose.*

9. Food Specialties of France

These expressions and names of dishes will be useful in restaurants or private homes where you may be invited. These dishes commonly appear on most French menus and are so much a part of the French dining tradition that you should recognize them on sight and know how to pronounce them as well as to enjoy them! We have written the French first, since that's how you will see it on the menu.

What is today's special?
Quel est le plat du jour?
kel ay luh pla-du-zhoor?

Is it ready?
Est-ce que c'est prêt?
ess-kuh say pray?

How long will it take?
Combien de temps faut-il attendre?
kohn-b'yen duh tahn fo-teel ah-tahndr'?

(une) Soupe à l'oignon	**(des) Escargots de Bourgogne**	**(des) Cuisses de Grenouille**
ůne soop ah lo n'yohn	*(day) zess-kar-go duh boor-goyn*	*(day) kweess duh gruh-nwee*
Onion soup	Snails with garlic	Frog legs

(la) Bouillabaisse	**(la) Sole aux Amandes**
(la) boo-ya-bayss	*(la) sol oh za-mahnd*
Fish and shellfish stew	Fillet of sole with almonds

(le) Vol au Vent
luh vohl oh vahn
Creamed chicken, sweetbreads, and mushrooms in a pastry shell

---

1. *Pronounce ů like ee* with your lips in a tight circle.
2. *zh* is like the *s* in measure.
3. *n* means a nasal "n," pronounced through the nose.

une Poule au pot
ûne pool oh po
Boiled chicken and
vegetables

un Pot-au-feu
un po-toh-fuh
Boiled beef and vegetables

(le) Boeuf Bourguignon
(luh) buhf boor-gheen-yohn
Beef stew with wine

(la) Quiche Lorraine
(la) keesh lo-rain
Omelet Pie with ham

(le) Ris de Veau Financière
(luh) ree duh vo fee-nahns-yair
Sweetbreads with rich sauce

(la) Cervelle de Veau
(la) sair-vel duh vo
Calf's brains

(le) Canard à l'Orange
(luh) ka-nar ah lo-rahnzh
Roast duck with orange sauce

(les) Tripes à la mode de Caen
(lay) treep ah la mod duh kahn
Tripe with tomatoes and
onions

(la) Tête de Veau Vinaigrette
(la) tait duh vo vee-nay-grett
Calf's head with vinegar
sauce

(une) Omelette Fines Herbes
(ûne) om-let feen-zairb
Omelet with chopped herbs

(la) Salade Niçoise
(la) sa-lahd nee-swahz
Lettuce, tomatoes, eggs,
anchovies, etc.

(les) Coquilles St. Jacques
(lay) ko-kee sen zhahk
Scallops and mushrooms in
cream sauce

(la) Blanquette de Veau
(la) blahn-kett duh vo
Veal with white wine sauce

(la) Tarte Alsacienne
(la) tart al-zass-yenn
Apple pie with custard

(les) Crêpes Suzette
(lay) krayp sû-zett
Pancakes with orange and
liqueur sauce

How do you like it?
Comment le trouvez-vous?
ko-mahn luh troo-vay-voo?

What is it?
Qu'est-ce que c'est?
kess kuh say?

It's delicious!
C'est délicieux!
say day-leess-yuh!

It's exquisite!
C'est exquis!
say tex-kee!

You have an excellent chef!
Vous avez un excellent chef!
*Voo za-vay un nek-sel-
lahn sheff!*

What an excellent cook!
Quelle excellente cuisinière!
*kel ek-sell-lahnt kwee-
zeen-yair!*

It was a great pleasure!
Comme c'était agréable!
kom say-tay ta-gray-ahbl'!

Thank you for a wonderful dinner!
Merci pour un dîner merveilleux!
mair-see poor un dee-nay mair-vay-yuh.

Don't mention it, sir.
Je vous en prie, monsieur.
zhuh voo zahn pree, muss-yuh.

En passant: The phrase **je vous en prie** is a typical French expression with various meanings, among which are "I beg you," "You first," "Think nothing of it," or "Please take this," depending on how it is used.

When you are offered something more and you say **Merci** —"Thank you"—it can mean "No, thanks." So if you do want to accept another helping, say "A little more, thank you"—**Encore un peu, merci** *(Ahn-kor un puh, mair-see).*

---

1. *Pronounce ŭ like ee with your lips in a tight circle.
2. *zh* is like the *s* in measure.
3. *n* means a nasal "n," pronounced through the nose.

10. Transportation

Getting around by public transportation is enjoyable not only for the new and interesting things you see, but also because of the opportunities you have for practicing French. To make your travels easier, use short phrases when speaking to drivers or others when you ask directions. And don't forget **Pardon, S'il vous plaît,** and **Merci.**

Bus

Where is the bus stop?
Où est l'arrêt d'autobus?
oo ay la-ray doh-toh-bŭss?

Do you go to the Rue de la Paix?
Allez-vous à la Rue de la Paix?
ah-lay voo za la rŭ duh la pay?

No; take number nine.
Non; prenez le numéro neuf.
nohn; pruh-nay luh nŭ-may-ro nuff.

How much is the fare?	**Where do you want to go?**
C'est combien?	Où allez-vous?
say kohn-b'yen?	*oo ah-lay voo?*

To the Place Vendôme.	**Is it far?**	**It's not far.**
Place Vendôme.	C'est loin?	Ce n'est pas loin.
plass vahn-dom.	*say lwen?*	*suh nay pa lwen.*

---

1. *Pronounce ŭ like ee with your lips in a tight circle.*
2. *zh is like the s in measure.*
3. *n means a nasal "n," pronounced through the nose.*

Will you tell me where to get off?
Voulez-vous me dire où je dois descendre?
voo-lay voo muh deer oo zhuh dwa day-sahndr'?

Get off here.
Descendez ici.
day-sahn-day ee-see.

En passant: You take a priority number from the bus stop post before you get on the bus. It saves discussion of who gets on first.

POINT TO THE ANSWER

To make sure that you understand the answer to the question you have asked, show the following section to the bus driver or conductor so that they can select the answer. The sentence in French after the arrow asks them to point out the answer.

Veuillez indiquer ci-dessous la réponse à ma question. Merci.

Là-bas.   **De ce côté-ci.**   **De ce côté-là.**
Over there.   This way.   That way.

De l'autre côté de la rue.   **Au coin.**
On the other side of the street.   At the corner.

A droite.   **A gauche.**   **Tout droit.**
To the right.   To the left.   Straight ahead.

Je ne sais pas.
I don't know.

Taxi

Where is the taxi stand?
Où est la station des taxis?
oo ay la sta-s'yohn day tahk-see?

Are you free?
Etes-vous libre?
ett-voo leebr'?

Where to?
Où allons-nous?
oo ah-lohn noo?

To this address.
À cette adresse.
ah set ah-dress.

Do you know where it is?
Savez-vous où ça se trouve?
sa-vay-voo oo sa suh troov?

Faster, please.
Plus vite, s'il
  vous plaît.
*Plŭ veet, seel
  voo play.*

I am in a hurry.
Je suis pressé.
*zhuh swee pray-
  say.*

Slow down.
Ralentissez.
Ra-lahn-tee-say.

Stop here.
Arrêtez ici.
ah-ray-tay ee-see.

At the corner.
Au coin.
oh kwen.

How much is it?
C'est combien?
say kohn-b'yen?

Wait for me, please.
Attendez-moi, s'il vous plaît.
*ah-tahn-day-mwa,
  seel voo play.*

---

1. *Pronounce ŭ like ee with your lips in a tight circle.*
2. *zh is like the s in measure.*
3. *n means a nasal "n," pronounced through the nose.*

I'll be back soon.
Je reviens tout de suite.
zhuh ruhv-yen tood sweet.

In five minutes.
Dans cinq minutes.
dahn senk mee-nüt.

How much is it by the hour?
C'est combien de l'heure?
say kohn-b'yen duh lurr?

. . . per kilometer?
. . . du kilomètre?
. . . dü kee-lo-metr'?

Call for me tomorrow.
Venez me chercher demain.
vuh-nay muh shair-shay duh-men.

POINT TO THE ANSWER

To make sure that you understand the answer to a question you have asked a taxidriver, show him or her the following section. The sentence in French after the arrow asks him or her to point to the answer.

 Veuillez indiquer ci-dessous la réponse à ma question. Merci.

Je vous attendrai ici.
I will wait for you here.

Je ne peux pas attendre.
I can't wait.

Je reviendrai vous prendre.
I'll be back to pick you up.

I can't park here.
Je ne peux pas stationner
    ici.

Ce n'est pas assez.
It is not enough.

Les bagages sont en plus.
The baggage is extra.

En passant: Tip 10% or 15% of the meter. After midnight there is a surcharge on the regular fare.

Subway

The subway	One first class.	Second class.
Le métro	Une première.	Deuxième classe.
luh may-tro	*ůne pruhm-yair.*	*duhz'yem klahss.*

Is it direct?	Must I change trains?
C'est direct?	Faut-il changer?
say dee-rekt?	*foh-teel shahn-zhay?*

Take the line (literally, the "direction") **to the Porte
    d'Italie.**
Prenez la direction Porte d'Italie.
pruh-nay ladee-reks-yohn port dee-ta-lee.

Change at Châtelet.
Changez au Châtelet.
shahn-zhay oh shat-lay.

Then take the "direction" _____ .
Puis prenez la direction _____ .
pwee pruh-nay la dee-reks-yohn _____ .

Get off at _____ .
Descendez à _____ .
day-sahn-day za _____ .

I took the wrong line.
Je me suis trompé de ligne.
zhuh muh swee trohn-pay duh leen.

Can you help me?	I want to go to _____ .
Pouvez-vous m'aider?	Je veux aller _____ .
poo-vay-voo may-day?	*zhuh vuh za-lay* _____ .

---

1. *Pronounce ů like ee* with your lips in a tight circle.
2. *zh* is like the *s* in measure.
3. *n* means a nasal "n," pronounced through the nose.

En passant: Lines are all separate and are called by the name of the stop where they *end.* You can change from one to the other at the points where they intersect, called **correspondances.** Each line has a map of its stops within the car, and each station has an understandable map of the whole subway system.

Train

Railroad
Chemin de fer
shuh-men duh fair

Where is the station?
Où est la gare?
oo ay la gahr?

Where does one buy tickets?
Où achète-t-on les billets?
oo a-shett-tohn lay bee-yay?

A ticket to Nice.
Un billet pour Nice.
un bee-yay poor neess.

One way only.
Aller seulement.
ah-lay suhl-mahn.

Round trip.
Aller retour.
ah-lay ruh-toor.

First class.
Première classe.
pruhm-yair klahss.

Second class.
Deuxième classe.
duhz'yem klahss.

A timetable.
Un indicateur.
un nen-dee-ka-turr.

Where is the train to _____ ?
Où est le train pour _____ ?
oo ay luh tran poor _____ ?

When do we leave?
Quand partons-nous?
kahn pahr-tohn-noo?

What track?
Quelle voie?
kel vwa?

Is this seat taken?
Est-ce que cette place est prise?
ess-kuh set plahss ay preez?

Will you allow me, madam?
Vous permettez, madame?
voo pair-may-tay, ma-dahm?

Go right ahead, sir.
Je vous en prie, monsieur.
zhuh voo zahn pree, muss-yuh.

What time do we get to Marseilles?
À quelle heure arrivons-nous à Marseille?
ah kel err ah-ree-vohn noo za mar-say?

Do we stop in Tours?
On s'arrête à Tours?
ohn sa-rett ah toor?

How long are we stopping here?
Combien de temps s'arrête-t-on ici?
kohn-b'yen duh tahn sa-rett-tohn ee-see?

Where is the dining car?
Où est le wagon restaurant?
ou ay luh va-gohn ress-toh-rahn?

I can't find my ticket.
Je ne trouve pas mon billet.
zhuh nuh troov pa mohn bee-yay.

Wait! Here it is.
Attendez! Le voici.
ah-tahn-day! luh vwa-see.

Please prepare my berth.
Préparez ma couchette, s'il vous plaît.
pray-pa-ray ma koo-shett, seel voo play.

---

1. *Pronounce* ü *like* ee *with your lips in a tight circle.*
2. *zh* is like the *s* in measure.
3. *n* means a nasal "n," pronounced through the nose.

En passant: Railroads, like the subways, have first and second class—**première** and **deuxième**. When the train goes across the border to Belgium, Germany, Spain, etc., customs and passport inspection takes place on the train.

POINT TO THE ANSWER

To make sure that you understand the answer to a question you have asked about trains, show the following section to a conductor or station guard so that they can select the answer. The sentence in French after the arrow asks them to point to the answer.

 Veuillez indiquer ci-dessous la réponse à ma question. Merci.

Le quai numéro _____ .   **En bas.**   **En haut.**
Track number _____ .   Downstairs.   Upstairs.

Ce n'est pas votre train.   **Celui-ci va à** _____ .
This is not your train.   This one goes to _____

Il faut changer à _____ .
You must change at _____ .

Nous arrivons à _____ **heures.**   **De ce côté-là.**
We arrive at _____ o'clock.   That way.

Le train part dans _____ **minutes.**
The train leaves in _____ minutes.

Ship

The ship.
Le bateau.
luh ba-toh.

To pier number six.
Au quai numéro six.
o kay nŭ-may-ro seess.

Where is my cabin?
Où est ma cabine?
oo ay ma ka-been?

Which deck?
Quel pont?
kell pohⁿ?

Are you the steward?
Etes-vous le steward?
ett-voo luh steward?

Where is the dining salon?
Où est la salle à manger?
oo ay la sa-la mahⁿ-zhay?

What time are meals served?
A quelle heure sert-on les repas?
ah kell err sair-tohⁿ lay ruh-pa?

At what time do we sail?
A quelle heure partons-nous?
ah kell err par-tohⁿ-noo?

Where is the purser?
Où est le commissaire?
oo ay luh ko-mee-sair?

---

1. *Pronounce* ŭ *like* ee *with your lips in a tight circle.*
2. *zh* is like the *s* in measure.
3. *ⁿ* means a nasal "n," pronounced through the nose.

I want to change tables.
Je voudrais changer de table.
zhuh voo-dray shahn-zhay duh tabl'.

(In Paris): At which pier are the sight-seeing boats?
A quel quai se trouvent les bateaux-mouches?
ah kel kay suh troov lay ba-toh-moosh?

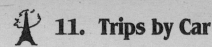

11. Trips by Car

Car Rental

The automobile.
L'automobile.
lo-toh-mo-beel.

Where can one rent a car?
Où peut-on louer une voiture?
oo puh-tohⁿ lway ůne vwa-tůr?

. . . a motorcycle?
. . . une motocyclette?
. . . ůne mo-toh-see-klett?

. . . a bicycle?
. . . une bicyclette?
. . . ůne bee-see-klett?

I want to rent a car.
Je voudrais louer une voiture.
zhuh voo-dray lway ůne vwa-tůr.

How much per day?
C'est combien par jour?
say kohⁿ-b'yeⁿ par zhoor?

How much per kilometer?
C'est combien du kilomètre?
*say kohⁿ-b'yeⁿ dů
        kee-lo-metr'?*

Is the gasoline included?
L'essence est comprise?
lay-sahⁿs ay kohⁿ-preez?

Is the transmission automatic?
Est-ce que le changement de vitesse est automatique?
ess-kuh luh shahⁿzh-mahⁿ duh vee-tess ay oh-toh-ma-teek?

I would like to try it out.
Je voudrais l'essayer.
zhuh voo-dray lay-say-yay.

En passant: Distances are reckoned in kilometers—approximately ⅝ of a mile.

---

1. *Pronounce* ů *like* ee *with your lips in a tight circle.*
2. *zh is like the* s *in measure.*
3. *ⁿ means a nasal* "n," *pronounced through the nose.*

Gas Station

Where can one buy gasoline?
Où peut-on acheter de l'essence?
oo puh-tohn ahsh-tay duh lay-sahns?

How much per liter?
C'est combien le litre?
say kohn-b'yen luh leetr'?

A hundred francs' worth of high test.
Cent francs de super.
Sahn frahn duh sŭ-pair.

Thirty liters, please.
Trente litres, s'il vous plaît.
trahnt leetr', seel voo play.

Fill it up.
Faites le plein.
fett luh plen.

Please—
S'il vous plaît—
seel voo play—

Put air in the tires.
Gonflez les pneus.
gohn-flay lay p'nuh.

Check . . .
Vérifiez . . .
vay-reef-yay . . .

. . . the water.
. . . l'eau.
. . . lo.

. . . the battery.
. . . la batterie.
. . . la batt-ree.

. . . the oil.
. . . l'huile.
. . . lweel.

. . . the spark plugs.
. . . les bougies.
. . . lay boo-zhee.

. . . the carburetor.
. . . le carburateur.
. . . luh car-bŭ-ra-turr.

. . . the brakes.
. . . les freins.
. . . lay fren.

Change the oil.
Changez l'huile.
shahn-zhay lweel.

Wash the car.
Lavez la voiture.
la-vay la vwa-tŭr.

Grease the motor.
Graissez le moteur.
gray-say luh mo-turr.

Change this tire.
Changez ce pneu.
shahn-zhay suh p'nuh.

A road map, please.
Une carte routière, s'il vous plaît.
ůne kart root-yair, seel voo play.

En passant: Gas is sold by the liter (1.05 quarts). In other words, 4 liters is about 1 gallon.

Asking Directions

Where does this road go to?
Où va ce chemin?
oo va suh shuh-men?

Is this the way to Chalons?
C'est bien la route de Chalons?
say b'yen la root duh sha-lohn?

Is the road good?
Est-ce que la route est bonne?
ess kuh la root ay bunn?

Which is the road to Epernay?
Quelle est la route d'Épernay?
kell ay la root day-pair-nay?

It's that way.
C'est par là.
say par la.

Is the next town far?
C'est loin la prochaine ville?
say lwen la pro-shen veel?

Is there a good restaurant there?
Y a-t-il un bon restaurant?
ee ya teel un bohn ress-toh-rahn?

---

1. *Pronounce ů like ee with your lips in a tight circle.*
2. *zh is like the s in measure.*
3. *n means a nasal "n," pronounced through the nose.*

Is there a good hotel in Tours?
Y a-t-il un bon hôtel à Tours?
ee ya teel un bohn o-tel ah toor?

POINT TO THE ANSWER

To make sure that you understand the answer to a question
you have asked about roads and directions, show the following section to a French-speaking person so that he or she
can select the answer.

> *Veuillez indiquer ci-dessous la réponse à ma*
> *question. Merci.*

Vous êtes ici sur la carte.   Suivez cette route-ci.
You are here on the map.   Follow this road.

La prochaine ville s'appelle _____ .
The next town is called _____ .

C'est ne pas loin.
It's not far.

Environ _____ kilomètres.
About _____ kilometers.

En sortant du village . . .
As you leave the village . . .

. . . tournez à droite au feu d'arrêt.
. . . turn right at the light.

Quand vous arrivez au pont . . .
When you come to the bridge . . .

. . . traversez-le,
. . . cross it,

prenez à droite   **. . . alors prenez à gauche.**
turn right   . . . then turn left.

Allez tout droit . . .
Go straight ahead . . .

jusqu'à l'autopiste.
up to the expressway.

Mais, attention!
But be careful!

Il y a une limite de vitesse.
There's a speed limit.

Emergencies and Repairs

Your license!
Votre permis de conduire!
votr' pair-mee duh kohn-dweer!

Here it is, officer.
Le voilà, monsieur l'agent.
luh vwa-la, muss-yuh la-zhahn.

And the registration (gray card).
Et la carte grise.
ay la cart greez.

---

1. *Pronounce ů like ee with your lips in a tight circle.*
2. *zh is like the s in measure.*
3. *n means a nasal "n," pronounced through the nose.*

It wasn't my fault.
Ce n'était pas ma faute.
suh nay-tay pa ma foht.

The truck skidded.
Le camion a dérapé.
luh kam-yohn ah day-ra-pay.

This imbecile crashed into me.
Cet imbécile m'est rentré dedans.
set en-bay-seel may rahn-tray duh-dahn.

En passant: As the French drive with considerable dash and challenge, **imbécile, idiot,** and **brute** are frequent and even rather mild expletives. However, control and good humor, plus a diplomatic use of French, will make driving safe and enjoyable.

I am in trouble
Je suis en difficulté.
zhuh swee zahn dee-fee-kŭl-tay.

Can you help me?
Pouvez-vous m'aider?
poo-vay-voo may-day?

My car has broken down.
Ma voiture est en panne.
ma vwa-tŭr ay tahn pahnn.

I have a flat tire.
J'ai un pneu à plat.
zhay un p'nuh ah pla.

Can you lend me a jack?
Pouvez-vous me prêter un cric?
poo-vay-voo muh pray-tay un kreek?

Can you push me?
Pouvez-vous me pousser?
poo-vay-voo muh poo-say?

Thank you very much.
Merci bien.
mair-see b'yen.

You are very kind.
Vous êtes très aimable.
voo zett tray zay-mabl'.

I would like to speak with the mechanic.
Je voudrais parler avec le mécanicien.
zhuh voo-dray par-lay ah-vek luh may-ka-nees-yen.

He doesn't work on the weekend.
Il ne travaille pas le weekend.
eel nuh tra-vye pa luh week-end.

The car doesn't run well.
Cette voiture ne marche pas bien.
set vwa-tŭr nuh marsh pa b'yen.

What is the matter?
Qu'est-ce qu'il y a?
kess-keel ee ya?

There's a noise in the motor.
Il y a un bruit dans le moteur.
eel ee ya un brwee dahn luh mo-turr.

The motor stalls.
Le moteur cale.
luh mo-turr kahl.

Difficult to start.
Difficile à démarrer.
dee-fee-seel ah day-ma-ray.

Can you fix it?
Pouvez-vous le réparer?
poo-vay-voo luh ray-pa-ray?

---

1. *Pronounce ŭ* like *ee* with your lips in a tight circle.
2. *zh* is like the *s* in measure.
3. *n* means a nasal "n," pronounced through the nose.

What will it cost?
Ce sera combien?
suh suh-ra kohn-b'yen?

How long will it take?
Combien de temps faut-il?
kohn-b'yen duh tahn fo-teel?

I'm in a hurry.
Je suis pressé.
Zhuh swee press-say.

En passant: For making sure exactly when the car will be
ready, consult the phrases in the "Time" section, page 25.
    Some English words, like "weekend," have been adopted
into French. "Cocktail," "business," "job," "cowboy,"
and "gangster" are other examples.

POINT TO THE ANSWER

To make sure that you understand the answer to a question
you have asked about car repairs, show the following section to the mechanic so that he or she can point to the
answer.

> *Veuillez indiquer ci-dessous la réponse à ma
> question. Merci.*

Ce sera prêt dans _____ heures.
It will be ready in _____ hours.

Ça va vous coûter _____ francs.
It will cost you _____ francs.

Aujourd'hui ce n'est pas possible.
Today isn't possible.

Peut-être demain.	**Demain, sûrement.**
Perhaps tomorrow.	Tomorrow, for sure

Après-demain.
The day after tomorrow.

Ce sera prêt dans _____ jours.
It will be ready in _____ days.

Nous n'avons pas la pièce de rechange.
We don't have the spare part.

Nous pouvons faire une réparation provisoire.
We can make a temporary repair.

Vous avez aussi besoin d'un pneu neuf.
You also need a new tire.

---

1. *Pronounce ů* like *ee* with your lips in a tight circle.
2. *zh* is like the *s* in measure.
3. *ⁿ* means a nasal "n," pronounced through the nose.

International Road Signs

Danger

Caution

Sharp turn

Crossroads

Right curve

Left curve

Guarded RR crossing

Unguarded RR crossing

Main road ahead

Bumps

One way

Do not enter

No parking

Parking

En passant: Did you notice that the bar on the international road signs means "Stop" or "Don't"? That is why we have made use of the barred *n* as the symbol for the typical French "nasal" sound in our phonetics—to show you that you don't really pronounce the *n* but say the vowel through your nose and then cut off your breath quickly.

In addition, you will hear or see the following instructions:

Maintenez votre droite.
men-tuh-nay votr' drwaht.
Keep to the right.

Ralentissez
ra-lahn-tee-say
Slow down

Détour
day-toor
Detour

Sens unique
sahns ŭ-neek
One way

Carrefour
kar-foor
Crossroads

Vitesse maximum _____ **km.**
vee-tess mak-see-mum _____ *kee-lo-metr'*
Maximum speed _____ kilometers per hour

Serrez à gauche.
say-ray ah gohsh.
Squeeze left.

Stationnement interdit
stass-yon-mahn an-tair-dee
No parking

Sens interdit
sahns an-tair-dee
Do not enter

Interdit aux cyclistes
an-tair-dee oh see-kleest
No bicycle riders

Piétons
p'yay-tohn
Pedestrians

Travaux
Tra-vo
Men at work

---

1. *Pronounce ŭ* like *ee* with your lips in a tight circle.
2. *zh* is like the *s* in measure.
3. *n* means a nasal "n," pronounced through the nose.

12. Sight-seeing and Photography

We have combined these two important sections since you will want to take pictures of what you are seeing. If you are taking pictures indoors, be sure to ask the custodian, **C'est permis?**—"Is it permitted?"

I need a guide.
J'ai besoin d'un guide.
zhay buh-zwen dun gheed.

Are you a guide?
Etes-vous guide?
ett-voo gheed?

Do you speak English?
Parlez-vous anglais?
par-lay-voo zahn-glay?

It doesn't matter.
Ça ne fait rien.
sah nuh fay r'yen.

I speak some French.
Je parle un peu français.
zhuh parl un puh frahn-say.

How much do you charge per hour?
Combien demandez-vous de l'heure?
kohn-b'yen duh-mahn-day-voo duh lurr?

How much per day?
Combien par jour?
kohn-b'yen par zhoor?

For two people?
Pour deux personnes?
poor duh pair-sonn?

A group of four?
Un groupe de quatre?
un groop duh katr'?

Do you have a car?
Avez-vous une voiture?
ah-vay-voo zŭne vwa-tŭr?

---

1. *Pronounce ŭ like ee* with your lips in a tight circle.
2. *zh* is like the *s* in measure.
3. *n* means a nasal "n," pronounced through the nose.

We would like to see _____ .
Nous voudrions voir _____ .
noo voo-dree-ohn vwahr _____ .

Where is the Arch of Triumph?
Où est l'Arc de Triomphe?
oo ay lark duh tree-ohnf?

Is that the Cathedral of Notre Dame?
Est-ce la cathédrale Notre-Dame?
ess la ka-tay-drahl nohtr'-dahm?

We want to go to the Louvre.
Nous voulons aller au Louvre.
noo voo-lohn za-lay oh loovr'.

To the Place de la Concorde.
Place de la Concorde.
plahss duh la kohn-kord.

To the opera.
A l'Opéra.
ah lo-pay-ra.

To the Bois Boulogne.
Au Bois de Boulogne.
oh bwah duh boo-loy'n.

To Versailles.
A Versailles.
ah vair-sye.

How beautiful!
Comme c'est beau!
kohm say bo!

Very interesting.
Très intéressant.
tray zen-tay-ray-sahn.

From what period is this?
C'est de quelle époque?
say duh kell ay-pok?

Louis XIV.
Louis XIV.
lwee cat-orze.

First Empire.
Premier Empire.
pruhm-yay ahn-peer.

Second Empire.
Second Empire.
suh-cohnd ahn-peer.

You are a very good guide.
Vous êtes un très bon guide.
*voo zett zun tray bohn
  gheed.*

Come again tomorrow.
Venez encore demain.
*vuh-nay zahn-kohr
  duh-men.*

At 9 a.m.
A neuf heures du matin.
ah nuh verr dů ma-ten.

And, if you don't have a guide:

May one enter?
Peut-on entrer?
puh-tohn nan-tray?

It is open.
C'est ouvert.
say too-vair.

It is closed.
C'est fermé.
say fair-may.

What are the visiting hours?
Quelles sont les heures de visite?
kell sohn lay zerr duh vee-zeet?

It opens at two o'clock.
Ça ouvre à deux heures.
sa oovr' ah duh zerr.

It's closed for repairs.
C'est fermé pour
  réparation.
*say fair-may poor
  ray-pa-ra-s'yohn.*

Can one take photos?
Peut-on prendre des photos?
puh-tohn prahndr' day fo-toh?

It is permitted.
C'est permis.
say pair-mee.

It is forbidden.
C'est défendu.
say day-fahn-dů.

Check your camera.
Pas d'appareil photographique.
pa dap-pa-ray fo-toh-gra-feek.

---

1. *Pronounce* ů *like* ee *with your lips in a tight circle.*
2. *zh is like the s in measure.*
3. *n means a nasal "n," pronounced through the nose.*

Leave your packages in the checkroom.
Laissez les paquets au vestiaire.
lay-say lay pa-kay oh vest-yair.

What is the admission?
C'est combien l'entrée?
say kohn-b'yen lahn-tray?

Five francs 50.
Cinq francs cinquante.
sank frahn sen-kahnt.

And for children?
Et pour les enfants?
ay poor lay zahn-fahn?

Admission is free.
L'entrée est libre.
lahn-tray ay leebr'.

Your ticket, please.
Votre billet, s'il vous plaît.
votr' bee-yay, seel voo play.

No smoking.
Défense de fumer.
day-fahns duh fŭ-may.

Follow me.
Suivez-moi.
swee-vay-mwa.

This way, please.
Par ici, s'il vous plaît.
par ee-see, seel voo play.

this castle
ce château
suh sha-toh

this palace
ce palais
suh pa-lay

this church
cette église
set ay-gleez

this monument
ce monument
suh mo-nŭ-mahn

this street
cette rue
set rŭ

this square
cette place
set plahss

What is it?
Qu'est-ce que c'est?
kess kuh say?

It's magnificent!
C'est magnifique!
say mahn-yee-feek!

It is very interesting!
C'est très intéressant!
say tray zen-tay-ray-sahn!

It's very old, isn't it?
C'est très ancien, n'est-ce pas?
say tray zahnss-yen, ness-pa?

This is for you.
Voilà pour vous.
vwa-la poor voo.

Here are some signs you may see in public places and their pronunciations and meanings.

Hommes	**Dames**
ohm	*dahm*
Men	Ladies
Entrée	**Sortie**
ahn-tray	*sohr-tee*
Entrance	Exit
Ouvert	**Fermé**
oo-vair	*fair-may*
Open	Closed
Vestiaire	**Renseignements**
vess-t'yair	*rahn-sayn-mahn*
Checkroom	Information
Heures de visite	**Toilettes**
err duh vee-zeet	*twa-lett*
Visiting hours	Rest rooms
Tirez	**Poussez**
tee-ray	*poo-say*
Pull	Push
Chaud	**Froid**
sho	*frwa*
Hot	Cold

---

1. *Pronounce ů like ee* with your lips in a tight circle.
2. *zh* is like the *s* in measure.
3. *n* means a nasal "n," pronounced through the nose.

Défense de fumer	Défense d'entrer	Défense d'afficher
day-fahns duh fü-may	*day-fahns dahn-tray*	*day-fahns da-fee-shay*
No smoking	No admittance	No sign posting

En passant: The term **Défense** in signs has the general connotation "no" or "Don't do it," so when you see it, don't walk on the grass, smoke, photograph, or do whatever you might be tempted to do.

Photography

Where is a camera shop?
Où y a-t-il un magasin de photos?
oo ee-ya-teel un ma-ga-zen duh fo-toh?

I would like a roll of film.
Je voudrais un rouleau de pellicule.
zhuh voo-dray zun roo-lo duh pay-lee-kül.

. . . in color.
. . . en couleur.
. . . ahn koo-lurr.

black and white.
noir et blanc.
nwahr ay blahn.

Movie film for my camera.
Un film pour ma caméra.
un film poor ma ka-may-ra.

This is to be developed.
Ceci est à développer.
suh-see ay ta day-vuh-lo-pay.

How much per print?
Combien chaque photo?
kohn-b'yen shahk fo-toh?

Two of each.
Deux de chaque.
duh duh shahk.

An enlargement.
Un aggrandissement.
un nah-grahn-dees-mahn.

About this size.
A peu près comme ceci.
ah puh pray kom suh-see.

When will it be ready?
Quand ce sera prêt?
kahn suh-suh-ra pray?

Flashbulbs.
Des ampoules flash.
day zahn-pool flahsh.

For this camera.
Pour cet appareil,
poor set ah-pa-ray.

Can you fix this?
Pouvez-vous réparer ceci?
poo-vay-voo ray-pa-ray suh-see?

It's broken.
C'est cassé.
say ka-say.

May one take photos here?
Peut-on prendre des photos ici?
puh-tohn prahndr' day fo-toh ee-see?

Pardon me, Miss,
Je m'excuse, Mademoiselle,
zhuh mek-skŭz, mahd-mwa-zell,

will you permit me
me permettez-vous
muh pair-may-tay-voo

to take a photo of you?
de prendre une photo de vous?
duh prahndr' ŭne fo-toh duh voo?

Stand here.
Mettez-vous là.
may-tay voo la

Don't move.
Ne bougez pas.
nuh boo-zhay pa.

Smile!
Souriez!
soo-ree-ay.

That's it!
C'est ça!
say sa.

Will you kindly take one of me?
Voulez-vous bien en prendre une de moi?
voo-lay-voo b'yen nahn prahndr' ŭne duh mwa?

In front of this door.
Devant cette porte.
duh-vahn set port.

You are very kind.
Vous êtes bien aimable.
voo zett b'yen nay mahbl'.

---

1. *Pronounce* ŭ *like* ee *with your lips in a tight circle.*
2. *zh is like the s in measure.*
3. n *means a nasal "n," pronounced through the nose.*

May I send you one?
Peut-on vous en envoyer une?
puh-tohn voo zahn nahn-vwah-yay ûne?

Your name?	**Your address?**
Votre nom?	Votre adresse?
votr' nohn?	*votr' ah-dress?*

POINT TO THE ANSWER

To make sure that you understand the answer to a question about cameras or film, show the following section to the employee of the *magasin de photos* so that he or she can select the answer.

 Veuillez indiquer ci-dessous la réponse à ma question. Merci.

Revenez demain.
Come back tomorrow.

A _____ heures.
At _____ o'clock.

Revenez dans _____ jours.
Come back in _____ days.

Nous pouvons le réparer.
We can repair it.

Nous ne pouvons pas le réparer.
We cannot repair it.

Nous n'en avons pas.
We haven't any.

Vous pouvez en trouver chez Kodak.
You can find some at Kodak.

En passant: Asking to take pictures of someone often leads to more general conversation. For this reason the following three sections will be especially interesting to you.

---

1. *Pronounce* ǔ like *ee* with your lips in a tight circle.
2. *zh* is like the *s* in measure.
3. *n* means a nasal ''n,'' pronounced through the nose.

13. Entertainment

This section shows you how to extend and accept invitations and suggest things to do, and it gives some typical conversations for theaters or nightclubs and some suitable words of appreciation when you are asked for dinner.

Things to Do

May I invite you . . .
Est-ce que je peux vous inviter . . .
ess kuh zhuh puh voo zen-vee-tay . . .

. . . to dinner?
. . . à dîner?
. . . ah dee-nay?

. . . to lunch?
. . . à déjeuner?
. . . ah day-zhuh-nay?

. . . to have a drink?
. . . à prendre un verre?
. . . ah prahn-dr' un vair?

. . . to dance?
. . . à danser?
. . . ah dahn-say?

. . . to go for a drive?
. . . à faire une promenade en voiture?
. . . ah fair ŭne prohm-nahd ahn vwah-tŭr?

. . . to play bridge?
. . . à jouer au bridge?
. . . ah zhoo-ay oh bridge?

. . . to the movies?
. . . au cinéma?
. . . oh see-nay-ma?

. . . to the theater?
. . . au théâtre?
. . . oh tay-ahtr'?

. . . to play golf?
. . . à jouer au golf?
. . . ah zhoo-ay oh gohlf?

---

1. *Pronounce ŭ like ee with your lips in a tight circle.*
2. *zh is like the s in measure.*
3. *n means a nasal "n," pronounced through the nose.*

. . . to play tennis?
. . . à jouer au tennis?
. . . *ah zhoo-ay oh tay-nees?*

Thank you very much.
Merci bien.
mair-see b'yen.

With pleasure.
Avec plaisir.
ah-vek play-zeer.

I am sorry.
Je regrette.
zhuh ruh-grett.

I cannot.
Je ne peux pas.
zhuh nuh puh pa.

I am busy.
Je suis occupé.
zhuh swee zo-kǔ-pay.

I am waiting for someone.
J'attends quelqu'un.
zha-tahn kel-kun.

I am tired.
Je suis fatigué.
zhuh swee fa-tee-gay.

I don't feel well.
Je ne me sens pas bien.
*zhuh nuh muh sahn pa
b'yen.*

Perhaps another time.
Peut-être une autre fois.
puh-tetr' ǔne oh-tr' fwa.

**Where are we going
tomorrow?**
Où allons-nous demain?
oo ah-lohn-noo duh-men?

Let's go . . .
Allons . . .
ah-lohn . . .

. . . around town.
. . . visiter la ville.
. . . vee-zee-tay la veel.

. . . to see a fashion show.
. . . voir une présentation de couture.
. . . *vwahr ǔne pray-zahn-tahs-yohn duh koo-tǔr.*

. . . to an art show.
. . . voir une exposition de peinture.
. . . *vwahr ǔne ex-po-zeess-yohn duh pen-tǔr.*

. . . to the film festival.
. . . au Festival du Film.
. . . *oh fes-tee-vahl dǔ film.*

. . . to the opera.
. . . à l'Opéra.
. . . *ah lo-pay-ra.*

. . . to see a new play.
. . . voir une nouvelle pièce.
. . . *vwahr ŭne noo-vel p'yess.*

. . . to the auto show.
. . . au Salon de l'Auto.
. . . *oh sa-lohn duh loh-toh.*

. . . to the meeting.
. . . à la réunion.
. . . *ah la ray-ŭn-yohn.*

. . . to the Flea Market.
. . . au Marché aux Puces.
. . . *oh mar-shay oh pŭss*

. . . to take a trip on the Seine.
. . . faire une promenade sur la Seine.
. . . *fair ŭne prom-nahd sŭr la sain.*

. . . to see a soccer game.
. . . voir un match de football.
. . . *vwahr un match duh foot-ball.*

. . . to the races.
. . . aux courses.
. . . *oh koors.*

Who is ahead?
Qui mène?
kee main?

Theaters and Nightclubs

What's playing?
Qu'est-ce qu'on joue?
kess kohn zhoo?

Two seats, please.
Deux places, s'il vous plaît.
duh plahss, seel voo play.

. . . in the orchestra.
. . . à l'orchestre.
. . . *a lohr-kestr'.*

---

1. *Pronounce* ŭ *like* ee *with your lips in a tight circle.*
2. *zh* is like the *s* in measure.
3. *n* means a nasal "n," pronounced through the nose.

. . . in the balcony.
. . . au balcon.
. . . oh bahl-kohn.

Are they good seats?
Ce sont de bonnes places?
suh sohn duh bunn plahss?

When does it start?
Quand commence-t-on?
kahn ko-mahnss-tohn?

What do you think of it?
Qu'est-ce que vous en pensez?
kess kuh voo zahn pahn-say?

It's very good.
C'est très bien.
say tray b'yen.

It's great!
C'est formidable!
say for-mee-dahbl'!

Who is playing the lead?
Qui joue le rôle principal?
*kee zhoo luh roll
pren-see-pal?*

She is beautiful.
Elle est belle.
ell ay bell.

It's very amusing.
C'est très amusant.
say tray za-mü-zahn.

Is it over?
C'est fini?
say fee-nee?

Let's go to a nightclub.
Allons dans un cabaret.
ah-lohn dahn zun ka-ba-ray.

A table near the dance floor.
Une table près de la piste.
üne tabl' pray duh la peest.

Is there a minimum charge?
Est-ce qu'il y a un tarif minimum?
ess keel ee ya un ta-reef mee-nee-mum?

For the first drink, 100 francs.
Pour la première consommation cent francs.
poor la pruhm-yair kohn-so-mahs-yon sahn frahn.

Shall we dance?
On danse?
ohn dahnss?

Shall we stay?
On reste?
ohn rest?

Let's leave.
Partons.
par-tohn.

An Invitation to Dinner

Can you come to dinner at our house?
Pouvez-vous venir dîner chez nous?
poo-vay-voo vuh-neer dee-nay shay noo?

. . . Monday at 8?
. . . lundi à huit heures?
. . . lun-dee ah wee terr?

With pleasure.
Avec plaisir.
ah-vek play-zeer.

If it isn't inconvenient for you.
Si ça ne vous dérange pas.
see sa nuh voo day-rahnzh-pa.

Very happy to see you.
Très content de vous voir.
tray kohn-tahn duh voo vwahr.

Sorry I'm late.
Je regrette d'être en retard.
zhuh ruh-gret detr' ahn ruh-tar.

The traffic was terrible!
La circulation était terrible!
la seer-kü-las'yohn ay-tay tair-reebl'!

Make yourself at home.
Faîtes comme chez vous.
fet kom shay voo.

What a beautiful house!
Quelle belle maison!
kell bell may-zohn!

Will you have something to drink?
Voulez-vous boire quelque chose?
voo-lay-voo bwahr kel-kuh shohz?

A cigarette?
Une cigarette?
üne see-ga-rett?

---

1. *Pronounce* ü *like* ee *with your lips in a tight circle.*
2. *zh is like the s in measure.*
3. *n means a nasal "n," pronounced through the nose.*

To your health!
A votre santé!
ah votr' sahn-tay!

Dinner is served.
Le dîner est servi.
luh dee-nay ay sair-vee.

Will you sit here?
Voulez-vous vous asseoir
  ici?
*voo-lay-voo voo za-swahr
  ee-see?*

What an excellent meal!
Quel excellent repas!
kel ek-say-lahn ruh-pa!

But have some more!
Mais reprenez-en!
may ruh-pruh-nay-zahn!

We had a wonderful time.
On s'est bien amusé.
ohn say b'yen na-mü-zay.

One (I, we) must go.
Il faut partir.
eel fo par-teer.

What a shame
Quel dommage!
kel doh-mazh!

I'll drive you back.
Je vais vous reconduire.
zhuh vay voo ruh-kohn-dweer.

No, please don't bother.
Non, je vous en prie, ne vous dérangez pas.
nohn, zhuh voo zahn pree, nuh voo day-rahn-zhay pa.

Thank you for your great hospitality.
Merci de votre bonne hospitalité.
mair-see duh votr' bunn oss-pee-ta-lee-tay.

But don't mention it.
Mais je vous en prie.
May zhuh voo zahn pree.

The pleasure was all ours.
Tout le plaisir était pour nous.
too luh play-zeer ay-tay poor noo.

En passant: You can get a lot of conversational mileage out of the expression **Il faut** followed by the infinitive of the verb (the form given in the dictionary). **Il faut** by context means either ''I must,'' ''One must,'' or ''You,'' ''he,'' ''she,'' ''it,'' ''we,'' or ''they must.'' The negative **ne . . . pas** fits around it—**Il ne faut pas**—''One must not,'' etc.

---

1. *Pronounce ǔ* like *ee* with your lips in a tight circle.
2. *zh* is like the *s* in measure.
3. *n* means a nasal ''n,'' pronounced through the nose.

14. Talking to People

Phrase books are generally too preoccupied with attending to your wants and the need for "getting along" to pay much attention to what you should say when you are introduced to someone. The following expressions have been tested for everyday conversational frequency and, except for the rather special ones at the end of the section, will be of immediate use for making conversation with anyone you may meet.

Do you live in this city?
Vous habitez cette ville?
voo za-bee-tay set veel?

Where are you from?
D'où êtes-vous?
Doo ett voo?

I am from Nancy.
Je suis de Nancy.
zhuh swee duh nahn-see.

Really?
Vraiment?
vray-mahn?

It's a beautiful city.
C'est une très belle ville.
say tǔne tray bel veel.

I've been there.
J'y ai été.
zhee yay ay-tay.

---

1. *Pronounce ǔ like ee with your lips in a tight circle.*
2. *zh is like the s in measure.*
3. *n means a nasal "n," pronounced through the nose.*

I would like to go there.
J'aimerais y aller.
zhaim-ray ee ah-lay.

How long have you been here?
Depuis quand êtes-vous ici?
duh-pwee kahn et-vóo zee-see?

For three days.
Depuis trois jours.
duh-pwee trwa zhoor.

Several weeks.
Quelques semaines.
kel-kuh suh-men.

Two months.
Deux mois.
duh mwa.

How long will you stay here?
Combien de temps allez-vous rester ici?
kohn-b'yen duh tahn ah-lay voo ress-tay ee-see?

I will stay _____ .
Je reste _____ .
zhuh rest _____ .

Have you been in France before?
Avez-vous déjà été en France?
ah-vay-voo day-zha ay-tay ahn frahnss?

No, never.
Non, jamais.
nohn, zha-may.

Yes, I've been here before.
Oui, j'y ai déjà été.
wee, zhee yay day-zha ay-tay.

Once.
Une fois.
ůne fwa.

Five years ago.
Il y a cinq ans.
eel ee ya seɴk ahɴ.

Where are you living?
Où habitez-vous?
oo ah-bee-tay-voo?

At what hotel?
A quel hôtel?
ah kel o-tel?

What do you think of Paris?
Comment trouvez-vous Paris?
ko-mahɴ troo-vay-voo pa-ree?

I like it very much.
Je l'aime beaucoup.
zhuh laim bo-koo.

It is very interesting.
C'est très intéressant.
say tray zeɴ-tay-ray-sahɴ.

The city is beautiful.
La ville est belle.
la veel ay bell.

The women are beautiful.
Les femmes sont belles.
lay fahm sohɴ bell.

Have you been in Normandy?
Avez-vous été en Normandie?
ah-vay voo zay-tay ahɴ nor-mahɴ-dee?

You must go there.
Il faut y aller.
eel fo tee ah-lay.

---

1. *Pronounce ů like ee with your lips in a tight circle.*
2. *zh is like the s in measure.*
3. *ɴ means a nasal "n," pronounced through the nose.*

En passant: When someone asks whether you have visited certain sections of France, you should be able to identify these areas by their regional names, which may not appear on a map and may be quite different from the English. Among these names are:

La Côte d'Azur
la koht da-zŭr
The Mediterranean coast of France

La Bourgogne
la boor-goy'n
Burgundy

Le Midi
luh mee-dee
The south of France

The names of the other sections resemble their English equivalents.

Les Châteaux de la Loire
lay sha-toh duh la lwahr
The chateaux of the Loire Valley

La Rive Gauche
la reev gohsh
The "Left Bank" (in Paris)

Are you from the United States?
Venez-vous des États-Unis?
vuh-nay-voo day zay-ta-zŭ-nee?

Yes, I am from San Francisco.
Oui, je suis de San Francisco.
wee, zhuh swee duh san francisco.

I speak French just a little.
Je parle français un tout petit peu.
zhuh parl frahn-say un too ptee puh.

But you have a good accent.
Mais vous avez un bon accent.
mais voo za-vay un bohn nakh-sahn.

You are very kind.
Vous êtes très aimable.
voo zett tray zay-mabl'.

Have you been to America?
Avez-vous été en Amérique?
ah-vay voo zay-tay ahn na-may-reek?

Where have you been?
Où avez-vous été?
oo ah-vay-voo zay-tay?

You must come to see us.	**At our house.**
Il faut venir nous voir.	Chez nous.
eel fo vuh-neer noo vwahr.	*shay noo.*

What do you think of _____ ?
Que pensez-vous de _____ ?
kuh pahn-say-voo duh _____ ?

Do you like _____ ?
Aimez-vous _____ ?
ay-may voo _____ ?

When people ask your opinion about something, you will find the following comments most helpful:

Magnificent.	**Wonderful.**
Magnifique.	Formidable.
mahn-yee-feek.	*for-mee-dabl'.*

---

1. *Pronounce ů like ee with your lips in a tight circle.*
2. *zh is like the s in measure.*
3. *n means a nasal "n," pronounced through the nose.*

Very interesting.
Très intéressant.
tray zeɴ-tay-ray-sahɴ.

Not bad.
Pas mal.
pa mahl.

Sometimes.
Quelquefois.
kel-kuh-fwa.

Often.
Souvent.
soo-vahɴ.

Once.
Une fois.
ůne fwa.

Never.
Jamais.
zha-may.

It seems to me that _____ .
Il me semble que _____ .
eel muh sahɴbl' kuh _____ .

In any case . . .
En tout cas . . .
ahɴ too ka . . .

It's a shame!
C'est dommage!
say doh-mazh!

I don't know.
Je ne sais pas.
zhuh nuh say pa.

I have forgotten.
J'ai oublié.
zhay oo-blee-yay.

I agree with you.
Je suis d'accord.
zhuh swee da-kor.

You are right.
Vous avez raison.
voo za-vay ray-zohɴ.

Are you married?
Etes vous marié?
ett voo mary-yay?

I am married.
Je suis marié.
zhuh swee mar-yay.

I am not married.
Je ne suis pas marié.
zhuh nuh swee pa mar-yay.

Is your wife here (there)?
Est-ce que votre femme est là?
ess kuh votr' fahm ay la?

Is your husband here (there)?
Est-ce que votre mari est
  là?
ess kuh votr' ma-ree ay la?

Do you have any children?
Avez-vous des enfants?
ah-vay voo day zahн-fahн?

Yes, I have.
Oui, j'en ai.
wee, zhahн nay.

No, I have not.
Non, je n'en ai pas.
nohн, zhuh nahн nay pa.

How many boys?
Combien de garçons?
kohн-b'yeн duh gar-sohн?

How many girls?
Combien de filles?
kohн-b'yeн duh fee?

How old are they?
Quel âge ont-ils?
kel azh ohн-teel?

My son is seven years old.
Mon fils a sept ans.
mohн fees ah set ahн.

**My daughter is ten years
  old.**
My fille a dix ans.
ma fee ya dee zahн.

What charming children!
Quels enfants charmants!
kel zahн-fahн shar-mahн!

Is it possible?
Est-ce possible?
ess po-seebl'?

Why not?
Pourquoi pas?
poor-kwa pa?

This is . . .	**. . . my . . .**	**. . . your . . .**
C'est . . .	. . . ma . . .	. . . votre . . .
say . . .	*. . . ma . . .*	*. . . votr' . . .*

---

1. *Pronounce* ŭ *like* ee *with your lips in a tight circle.*
2. *zh is like the* s *in measure.*
3. *н means a nasal "n," pronounced through the nose.*

... his (or her) ...   ... mother.
... sa ...   ... mère.
... *sa* ...   ... *mair.*

... sister.   ... wife.   ... daughter.
... soeur.   ... femme.   ... fille.
... *serr.*   ... *fahm.*   ... *fee.*

... daughter-in-law.   ... granddaughter.
... belle-fille.   ... petite-fille.
... *bell-fee.*   ... *puh-teet-fee.*

This is ...   ... my ...   ... your ...
C'est ...   ... mon ...   ... votre ...
say ...   ... *mohn* ...   ... *votr'* ...

... his (or her) ...   ... father.
... son ...   ... père.
... *sohn* ...   ... *pair.*

... brother.   ... husband.   ... son.
... frère.   ... mari.   ... fils.
... *frair.*   ... *ma-ree.*   ... *feess.*

... son-in-law.   ... grandson.
... beau-fils.   ... petit-fils.
... *bo-feess.*   ... *puh-tee-feess.*

Do you know ...   ... that man?
Connaissez-vous ...   ... cet homme?
ko-nay-say-voo ...   ... *set ohm?*

He is ...   ... a writer.
C'est ...   ... un écrivain.
say ...   ... *tun ay-kree-ven.*

... an artist.   ... an actor.
... un artiste.   ... un acteur.
... *tun nar-teest.*   ... *tun nahk-turr.*

. . . **a businessman.**
. . . un homme d'affaires.
. . . *tuꞃ nohm da-fair.*

. . . **a lawyer.**
. . . un avocat.
. . . *tuꞃ na-vo-ka.*

. . . **a banker.**
. . . un banquier.
. . . *tuꞃ
   bahꞃk-yay.*

. . . **a manufacturer.**
. . . un fabricant.
. . . *tuꞃ fa-bree-kahꞃ.*

. . . **a doctor.**
. . . un médecin.
. . . *tuꞃ maid-seꞃ.*

. . . **a professor.**
. . . un professeur.
. . . *tuꞃ pro-fay-surr.*

. . . **a military man.**
. . . un militaire.
. . . *tuꞃ mee-lee-tair.*

The "t" in front of "un" comes from the final "t" of *c'est*. This linkage is called *liaison*.

. . . **a politician.**
. . . un homme de politique.
. . . *tuꞃ nohm duh
   po-lee-teek.*

. . . **my husband.**
. . . mon mari.
. . . *mohꞃ ma-ree.*

Do you know . . .
Connaissez-vous . . .
ko-nay-say-voo . . .

. . . **that lady?**
. . . cette dame?
. . . *sett dahm?*

She is . . .
C'est . . .
say . . .

. . . **a singer.**
. . . une chanteuse.
. . . *tůne shahn-tuhz.*

---

1. *Pronounce* ů *like* ee *with your lips in a tight circle.*
2. *zh is like the s in measure.*
3. *ꞃ means a nasal "n," pronounced through the nose.*

. . . an actress.
. . . une actrice.
. . . *tŭne ak-treess*.

. . . my wife.
. . . ma femme.
. . . *ma fahm*.

Artist, writer, professor, doctor, and certain other professions are the same for masculine and feminine.

He is American.
Il est américain.
eel ay ta-may-ree-ken.

She is American.
Elle est américaine.
el ay ta-may-ree-kain.

He is French.
Il est français.
eel ay frahn-say.

She is French.
Elle est française.
el ay frahn-sayz.

He is German.
Il est allemand.
eel ay tahl-mahn.

She is German.
Elle est allemande.
el ay tahl-mahnd.

He is English.
Il est anglais.
eel ay tahn-glay.

She is English.
Ell est anglaise.
el ay tahn-glayz.

He is Canadian.
Il est canadien.
eel ay ka-nahd-yen.

She is Canadian.
Elle est canadienne.
el ay ka-nahd-yen.

He is Italian.
Il est italien.
eel ay tee-tal-yen.

She is Italian.
Elle est italienne.
el ay tee-tal-yen.

Very nice.
Très sympathique.
tray sen-pa-teek.

Very intelligent.
Très intelligent. (m)
  Très intelligente. (f)
tray zen-tay-lee-zahn.
  tray zen-tay-lee-zhahnt.

Very pretty.
Très jolie. (f)
tray zho-lee.

Very capable.
Très capable.
tray ka-pabl'.

Here is my address.
Voici mon adresse.
vwa-see mohn na-dress.

What is your address?
Quelle est votre adresse?
kel ay votr' ah-dress?

Here is my telephone number.
Voici mon numéro de téléphone.
vwa-see mohn nŭ-may-ro duh tay-lay-fohn.

What is your telephone number?
Quel est votre numéro de téléphone?
kel ay votr' nŭ-may-ro duh tay-lay-fohn?

May I call you?
Est-ce que je peux vous appeler?
ess kuh zhuh puh voo zap-lay?

When?
Quand?
kahn?

Tomorrow morning.
Demain matin.
duh-men ma-ten.

Early.
De bonne heure.
duh bunn err.

Late in the afternoon.
En fin d'après-midi.
ahn fen da-pray-mee-dee.

Where?
Où?
oo?

What is your first name?
Quel est votre prénom?
kel ay votr' pray-nohn?

Mine is Richard.
Le mien, c'est Richard.
luh m'yen, say ree-shar.

You are very pretty.
Vous êtes très jolie.
voo zett tray zho-lee.

You are very kind.
Vous êtes bien aimable.
voo zett b'yen nay-mabl'.

You dance very well.
Vous dansez très bien.
voo dahn-say tray b'yen.

You sing very well.
Vous chantez très bien.
voo shahn-tay tray b'yen.

---

1. *Pronounce* ŭ *like* ee *with your lips in a tight circle.*
2. *zh* is like the *s* in measure.
3. *n* means a nasal "n," pronounced through the nose.

What a pretty dress!
Quelle jolie robe!
kel zho-lee rohb!

Do you think so?
Vous trouvez?
voo troo-vay?

I have a surprise for you.
J'ai une surprise pour vous.
zhay ůne sůr-preez poor voo.

Do you like it?
Ça vous plaît?
sa voo play?

Can we see each other again?
Est-ce que nous pouvons nous revoir?
ess kuh noo poo-vohn noo ruh-vwahr?

What's the matter?
Qu'est-ce qu'il y a?
kess keel ya?

Are you angry?
Etes-vous fâché? (-e)
ett-voo fa-shay?

Why?
Pourquoi?
poor-kwa?

I'm very sorry.
Je suis désolé.
zhuh swee day-zo-lay.

Where are you going?
Où allez-vous?
oo ah-lay voo?

Let's go together.
Allons-y ensemble.
ah-lohn zee ahn-sahnbl'.

You are very beautiful. (f.)
Vous êtes très belle.
voo zett tray bell.

You are very nice.
Vous êtes très sympathique.
voo zett tray sen-pa-teek.

What do you think of me?
Qu'est-ce que vous pensez de moi?
kess kuh voo pahn-say duh mwa?

I like you very much.
Vous me plaisez beaucoup.
voo muh play-zay bo-koo.

Really?
Vraiment?
vray-mahn?

No fooling?
Sans blague?
sahn blahg?

Will you give me your photo?
Voulez-vous me donner une photo?
voo-lay voo muh doh-nay ûne fo-toh?

Will you write me?
Est-ce que vous m'écrirez?
ess-kuh voo may-kree-ray?

Of course!
Bien entendu!
b'yen entendû!

I won't forget you.
Je ne vous oublierai pas.
zhuh nuh voo zoo-blee-ray pa.

I love you.
Je vous aime.
zhuh voo zaim.

---

1. *Pronounce û* like *ee* with your lips in a tight circle.
2. *zh* is like the *s* in measure.
3. *n* means a nasal "n," pronounced through the nose.

15. Words That Show You Are "With It"

There are certain words constantly used by French people that do not have an exact equivalent in English. To use them at the right time will indicate to French-speaking people that you have good manners and are familiar with the most frequently used French conversational phrases—in other words, that you are "with it."

We have divided these phrases into two groups. The first is composed of selected polite expressions:

Bravo!
bra-vo!
Good (for you)!

Bon voyage!
bohn vwa-yazh!
Have a good trip!

Bon séjour!
bohn say-zhoor!
Have a good stay!

Faites comme chez vous!
fett kom shay voo!
Make yourself at home!

A votre santé!
ah votr' sahn-tay!
To your health!

Mes compliments!
may kohn-plee-mahn!
My compliments!

Mes amitiés à _____
may za-meet-yay ah _____
My regards to _____

Bon appétit!
bohn na-pay-tee!
Good appetite!

Amusez-vous bien!
ah-mŭ-zay-voo b'yen!
Have a good time!

Au plaisir.
oh play-zeer.
Good-bye. (very polite)

---

1. *Pronounce* ŭ like *ee* with your lips in a tight circle.
2. *zh* is like the *s* in measure.
3. *n* means a nasal "n," pronounced through the nose.

Félicitations.
fay-lee-see-tahss-yohn.
Congratulations!

Bonne chance!
bunn shahnss!
Good luck!

Because the following phrases occur frequently in conversation, it will interest you to know what they mean, as well as to learn to use them as conversational stopgaps. The translations are rather free, as these expressions are very idiomatic.

Je vous en prie.
zhuh voo zahn pree.
Please do so (or)
  You are welcome.

Ce n'est rien.
suh nay r'yen.
It's really nothing.

Allez-y!   **Donc . . .**
ah-lay zee!   *dohnk . . .*
Go right ahead!   Then . . .

Voyons.
vwa-yohn.
Let's see.

Entendu . . .
ahn-tahn-dü . . .
It's understood . . .

D'accord.
da-kor.
I agree. (It's agreed.)

Mon Dieu!
mohn d'yuh!
Heavens! (My God!)

Allons donc.
ah-lohn dohnk.
Well, now.

Formidable!
for-mee-dahbl'!
Just great! Remarkable!

N'est-ce pas?
ness pa?
Isn't it! (Isn't that right?)

Ça va?
sa va?
Is it all right?
  (How's it going?)

Ça va.
sa va.
It's all right.
  (It's going fine.)

Quand même.
kahn mem.
Well, really! (In any
  case . . .)

Eh bien . . .
eh b'yen . . .
Well . . .

Alors . . .
ah-lor . . .
Then (or) and then what?

Quoi?
kwa?
What?

Ne vous en faites pas.
nuh voo zahn fett pa.
Don't worry about it.

Comment?
ko-mahn?
How's that?

Ce n'est pas la peine.
suh nay pa la pain.
It's not worth the trouble.

A la bonne heure!
ah la bunn nerr!
Fine! That's great!

Figurez-vous!
fee-gŭ-ray-voo!
Just imagine!

N'importe quoi.
nen-port kwa.
Anything at all.

Ça m'est égal.
sa may tay-gahl.
It's all the same to me.

Ça y est!
sa ee ay!
That's it!

Ne vous dérangez pas!
nuh voo day-rahn-zhay pa!
Don't bother!

Après tout . . .
ah-pray too . . .
After all . . .

Il me semble que . . .
eel muh senble kuh . . .
It seems to me that . . .

On dit que . . .
ohn dee kuh . . .
They say that . . .

C'est incroyable!
say tan-croy-ahbl'!
It's unbelievable!

Que voulez-vous?
kuh voo-lay-voo?
What do you expect?

C'est la vie.
say la vee.
That's life.

---

1. *Pronounce ŭ like ee with your lips in a tight circle.*
2. *zh is like the s in measure.*
3. *n means a nasal "n," pronounced through the nose.*

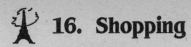

16. Shopping

Shops in France still tend to be specialized, although there exist chains of general stores and even the supermarket—supermarché.

Names of Shops

Where can one find . . .
Où peut-on trouver . . .
oo puh-tohн troo-vay . . .

. . . a department store?
. . . un grand magasin?
. . . uн grahн ma-ga-zeн?

. . . a dress shop?
. . . une maison de couture?
. . . ůne may-zohн duh koo-tůr?

. . . a hat shop?
. . . une modiste?
. . . ůne mo-deest?

. . . a shoe store?
. . . un magasin de chaussures?
. . . uн ma-ga-zeн duh sho-sůr?

. . . a jewelry shop?
. . . une bijouterie?
. . . ůne bee-zhoo-tree?

. . . a drugstore?
. . . une pharmacie?
. . . ůne far-ma-see?

. . . a bookshop?
. . . une librairie?
. . . ůne lee-bray-ree?

. . . a toy shop?
. . . un magasin de jouets?
. . . uн ma-ga-zeн duh zhoo-ay?

. . . an antique shop?
. . . un antiquaire?
. . . uн nahн-tee-kair?

---

1. *Pronounce ů like ee* with your lips in a tight circle.
2. *zh* is like the *s* in measure.
3. *н* means a nasal "n," pronounced through the nose.

101

. . . a flower shop?	. . . a bakery?
. . . un fleuriste?	. . . une boulangerie?
. . . *un fluh-reest?*	. . . *ûne boo-lahn-zhuh-ree?*

. . . a grocery store?
. . . un magasin d'alimentation?
. . . *un ma-ga-zen da-lee-mahn-tas-yohn?*

. . . a camera shop?	. . . a market?
. . . un magasin de photographie?	. . . un marché?
. . . *un ma-ga-zen duh fo-toh-gra-fee?*	. . . *un mar-shay?*

. . . a perfume shop?	. . . a tobacco shop?
. . . une parfumerie?	. . . un bureau de tabac?
. . . *ûne par-fû-muh-ree?*	. . . *un bû-ro duh ta-ba?*

. . . a barbershop?	. . . a beauty shop?
. . . un coiffeur?	. . . un salon de beauté?
. . . *un kwa-fur?*	. . . *un sa-lohn duh bo-tay?*

En passant: Although **magasin** is the usual word for "shop," **boutique** is also very much in use. On shop signs you will sometimes see the word **chez** followed by a name. **Chez Marcelle,** for example, means "At Marcelle's."

General Shopping Vocabulary

May I help you?	**What do you wish?**
Puis-je vous aider?	Vous désirez?
pweezh voo zay-day?	*voo day-zee-ray?*

I would like to buy . . .
Je voudrais acheter . . .
zhuh voo-dray zash-tay . . .

. . . a present for my husband.
. . . un cadeau pour mon mari.
. . . uɴ ka-do poor mohɴ ma-ree.

. . . a present for my wife.
. . . un cadeau pour ma femme.
. . . uɴ ka-do poor ma fahm.

. . . something for a man.
. . . quelque chose pour un homme.
. . . kel-kuh shohz poor uɴ nohm.

. . . for a girl.
. . . pour une jeune fille.
. . . poor ůne zhuhn fee.

. . . for a lady.
. . . pour une dame.
. . . poor ůne dahm.

Nothing for the moment.
Rien pour le moment.
r'yeɴ poor luh mo-mahɴ.

I'm just looking around.
Je regarde seulement.
zhuh ruh-gard suhl-mahɴ.

I'll be back later.
Je reviens plus tard.
zhuh ruh-v'yeɴ plů tar.

I like this.   **. . . that.**
J'aime ceci.   . . . cela.
zhaim suh-see.   *. . . suh-la.*

How much is it?
C'est combien?
say kohɴ-b'yeɴ?

Show me another.
Montrez-m'en un autre.
mohɴ-tray mahɴ uɴ notr'.

Something less expensive.
Quelque chose de moins cher.
kel-kuh shohz duh mweɴ shair.

---

1. *Pronounce* ů *like* ee *with your lips in a tight circle.*
2. *zh is like the s in measure.*
3. *ɴ means a nasal "n," pronounced through the nose.*

Do you like this?
Aimez-vous cela?
ay-may-voo suh-la?

May I try it on?
Est-ce que je peux l'essayer?
ess kuh juh puh lay-say-yay?

That suits you marvelously.
Ça vous va à merveille.
sa voo va ah mair-vay.

Can you alter it?
Pouvez-vous arranger cela?
poo-vay-voo zah-rahn-zhay suh-la?

Is it handmade?
Est-ce que c'est fait à la main?
ess kuh say fay ta la men?

. . . hand-embroidered?
. . . brodé à la main?
. . . bro-day ah la men?

Good, I'll take it.
Bon, je le prends.
bohn, zhuh luh prahn.

Can one pay by check?
On peut payer par chèque?
ohn puh pay-yay par shek?

The change, please.
La monnaie, s'il vous plaît.
la mo-nay, seel voo play.

A receipt, please.
Un reçu, s'il vous plaît.
un ruh-sù, seel voo play.

Will you wrap it?
Voulez-vous l'emballer?
voo-lay-voo lahn-ba-lay?

Can you send it?
Pouvez-vous l'expédier?
poo-vay-voo lex-paid-yay?

. . . to this address?
. . . à cette adresse?
. . . ah set ah-dress?

Come see us again!
Revenez nous voir!
ruh-vuh-nay noo vwahr!

On sale.
En solde.
ahn sold.

Bargain sale.
Solde d'occasions.
sold do-kaz-yohn.

POINT TO THE ANSWER

To make sure that you understand the answer to a question you have asked about shopping, show the following section to the salesperson so that he or she can select the answer.

 Veuillez indiquer ci-dessous la réponse à ma question. Merci.

Nous n'en avons pas.
We haven't any.

Nous n'avons rien de plus grand.
We haven't anything larger.

Nous n'avons rien de plus petit.
We haven't anything smaller.

Nous ne livrons pas.
We don't deliver.

Nous pouvons l'envoyer à une adresse en Amérique.
We can send it to an address in America.

Quelle est votre adresse?
What is your address?

---

1. *Pronounce* ŭ *like* ee *with your lips in a tight circle.*
2. *zh is like the s in measure.*
3. *n̶ means a nasal "n," pronounced through the nose.*

**Nous regrettons, mais nous ne pouvons pas accepter de
chèque à votre nom.**
We are sorry, but we cannot accept personal checks.

Nous acceptons des "traveler's checks."
We accept traveler's checks.

Clothes

a blouse un corsage *un kor-sazh*	**a skirt** une jupe *ůne zhůp*	**a woman's suit** un tailleur *un ta-yuhr*
a coat un manteau *un mahn-to*	**a hat** un chapeau *un sha-po*	**a scarf** une écharpe *ůne ay-sharp*
a handbag un sac *un sak*	**shoes** des chaussures *day sho-sůr*	**stockings** des bas *day ba*
gloves des gants *day gahn*	**pajamas** un pyjama *un pee-zha-ma*	**a nightgown** une chemise de nuit *ůne shuh-meez duh nwee*
a slip une combinaison *ůne kohn-bee- nay-sohn*	**panties** une culotte *ůne ků-loht*	**a brassiere** un soutien-gorge *un soot-yen gorzh*

slippers des pantoufles *day pahn-toofl'*	**a bathrobe** un peignoir de bain *un pay-nwahr duh ben*
an evening dress une robe du soir *ůne rohb dů swahr*	**an evening coat** un manteau du soir *un mahn-to dů swahr*

a raincoat
un imperméable
un nan-pair-may-ahbl'

boots
des bottes
day boht

an umbrella
un parapluie
un pa-ra-plwee

a swimsuit
un costume de bain
un kos-tǔme duh ben

a shirt
une chemise
ǔne shuh-meez

pants
un pantalon
un pahn-ta-lohn

a jacket
une veste
ǔne vest

a suit
un complet
un kohn-play

a tie
une cravate
ǔne kra-vaht

socks
des chaussettes
day sho-set

undershirt
un sous-vêtement
un soo-vet-mahn

undershorts
un caleçon
un kahl-sohn

swim trunks
un maillot de bain
un ma-yo duh ben

handkerchiefs
des mouchoirs
day moo-shwahr

Sizes—Colors—Materials

What size?
Quelle taille?
kell tye?

small
petit
puh-tee

medium
moyen
mwa-yen

large
grand
grahn

extra large
très grand
tray grahn

larger
plus grand
plǔ grahn

---

1. *Pronounce* ǔ like *ee* with your lips in a tight circle.
2. *zh* is like the *s* in measure.
3. *n* means a nasal ''n,'' pronounced through the nose.

smaller	wider	narrower
plus petit	plus large	plus étroit
plŭ puh-tee	*plŭ larzh*	*plŭ zay-trwa*

longer	shorter
plus long	plus court
plŭ lohn	*plŭ koor*

What color?	red	blue
De quelle couleur?	rouge	bleu
duh kell koo-lŭhr?	*roozh*	*bluh*

yellow	orange	green	purple
jaune	orange	vert	violet
zhohn	*o-rahnzh*	*vàir*	*vee-o-lay*

brown	gray	tan	black
brun	gris	beige	noir
brun	*gree*	*bayzh*	*nwahr*

white	darker	lighter
blanc	plus foncé	plus clair
blahn	*plŭ fohn-say*	*plŭ klair*

Is it silk?	wool	linen
C'est de la soie?	de la laine	du lin
say duh la swah?	*duh la lain*	*dŭ lan*

cotton	lace	velvet
du coton	de la dentelle	du velours
dŭ ko-tohn	*duh la dahn-tel*	*dŭ vuh-loor*

leather	suede	kid	plastic
du cuir	du daim	du chevreau	du plastique
dŭ kweer	*dŭ dan*	*dŭ shuh-vro*	*dŭ plahss-teek*

fur	What kind of fur?
de la fourrure	Quelle genre de fourrure?
duh la foo-rŭr	*kell zhahnr' duh foo-rŭr?*

fox	beaver	mink
du renard	du castor	du vison
dŭ ruh-nahr	*dŭ kahss-tohr*	*dŭ vee-zohn*

sable	Persian lamb
de la zibeline	de l'astrakan
duh la zeeb-leen	*duh lahss-tra-kahn*

Newsstand

I would like a guide book.
Je voudrais un guide.
zhuh voo-dray zun gheed.

a map of the city.
un plan de la ville.
un plahn dŭh la veel

postcards
des cartes postales
day kart pohs-tahl

sunglasses
des lunettes de soleil
day lŭ-net duh so-lay'

this newspaper
ce journal-ci
suh zhoor-nahl-see

that magazine
ce magazine-là
suh ma-ga-zeen-la

a newspaper in English
un journal en anglais
un zhoor-nahl ahn nahn-glay

Tobacco Shop

Have you American cigarettes?
Avez-vous des cigarettes américaines?
ah-vay voo day see-ga-ret ah-may-ree-kain?

---

1. *Pronounce ŭ* like *ee* with your lips in a tight circle.
2. *zh* is like the *s* in measure.
3. *n* means a nasal "n," pronounced through the nose.

Okay.	I'll take Gauloises.
Ça va.	Je prends des Gauloises.
sa va.	*zhuh prahn day go-lwahz.*

cigars	a pipe	tobacco
des cigares	une pipe	du tabac
day see-gar	*ůne peep*	*dů ta-ba*

matches	a lighter	a lighter refill
des allumettes	un briquet	un rechange
day zah-lů-met	*un bree-kay*	*un ruh-shahnzh*

Drugstore

a toothbrush	toothpaste	a razor
une brosse à dents	du dentifrice	un rasoir
ůne brohss ah dahn	*dů dahn-tee-freess*	*un ra-zwahr*

razor blades	shaving cream
des lames de rasoir	de la crème à raser
day lahm duh ra-zwahr	*duh la kraim ah ra-zay*

cologne	a hairbrush	a comb
de l'eau de Cologne	une brosse à cheveux	un peigne
duh lo duh ko-loy'n	*ůne brohss ah shuh-vuh*	*un pain*

aspirin	iodine	an antiseptic
de l'aspirine	de la teinture d'iode	un antiseptique
duh lahs-pee-reen	*duh la tan-tůr dee-ohd*	*un ahn-tee-sep-teek*

scissors	a nail file	a bandage
des ciseaux	une lime à ongles	des bandages
day see-zo	*ůne leem ah ohngl'*	*day bahn-dazh*

cough drops
des pastilles pour la toux
day pahs-tee poor la too

Cosmetics

makeup base	powder	lipstick
un fond de teint	de la poudre	un rouge à lèvres
un fohn duh ten	*duh la poodr'*	*un roozh ah levr'*

eye shadow	mascara
un crayon à paupières	du mascara
un kray-yohn ah pohp-yair	*dů mas-ka-ra*

eyebrow pencil	cleansing cream
un crayon à sourcils	de la crème à nettoyer
un kray-yohn ah soor-see	*duh la kraim ah nay-twah-yay*

bobby pins	cotton pads
des barrettes	des boules de coton
day ba-rett	*day bool duh koh-tohn*

perfume	That smells good, doesn't it?
du parfum	Ça sent bon, n'est-ce pas?
dů par-fen	*sa sahn bohn, ness pa?*

---

1. *Pronounce ů like ee with your lips in a tight circle.*
2. *zh is like the s in measure.*
3. *n means a nasal "n," pronounced through the nose.*

Hairdresser

a shampoo	**and set**	**a color rinse**
un shampooing	et mise en plis	un rinçage
un shahn-pwen	*ay mee-zahn plee*	*un ran-sahzh*

lighter	**darker**	**That's good.**
plus clair	plus foncé	Ça va.
plů klair	*plů fohn-say*	*sa va.*

a manicure	**a pedicure**
une manucure	une pédicure
ůne ma-nů-kůr	*ůne pay-dee-kůr*

Barber

a haircut	**a shave**	**a massage**
une coupe de cheveux	la barbe	un massage
ůne koop duh shuh-vuh	*la bahrb*	*un ma-sazh*

Use scissors.	**Not the clippers.**
Employez les ciseaux.	Pas là tondeuse.
ahn-plwa-yay lay see-zo.	*pa la tohn-duhz.*

shorter	**not too short**	**the top**
plus court	pas trop court	le dessus
plů koor	*pa tro koor*	*luh duh-sů*

in back	**the sides**	**That's fine.**
derrière	les côtés	C'est très bien.
dair-yair	*lay ko-tay*	*say tray b'yen.*

Food Market

I would like . . .
Je voudrais . . .
zhuh voo-dray . . .

. . . a dozen of . . .
. . . une douzaine de . . .
. . . ůne doo-zain duh . . .

. . . this.
. . . ceci.
. . . suh-see.

. . . that.
. . . cela.
. . . suh-la.

I want five.
J'en veux cinq.
zhahн vuh senk.

Is this fresh?
C'est bien frais?
say b'yeн fray?

Three cans of this.
Trois boîtes de ceci.
trwah bwaht duh suh-see.

How much per kilo?
C'est combien le kilo?
say kohн-b'yeн luh kee-lo?

Can one buy wine here?
Peut-on acheter du vin ici?
puh-tohн ash-tay dů vaн ee-see?

Brandy?
Du cognac?
dů kohn-yak?

What is this?
Qu'est-ce que c'est?
kess kuh say?

Put it in a bag, please.
Mettez-le dans un sac, s'il vous plaît.
may-tay-luh dahн zuн sak, seel voo play.

En passant: Wine and other alcoholic beverages are generally sold in food stores. **Une bonne idée, n'est-ce pas?**

---

1. *Pronounce ů* like *ee* with your lips in a tight circle.
2. *zh* is like the *s* in measure.
3. *н* means a nasal "n," pronounced through the nose.

Jewelry

I would like . . .	. . . a watch.	. . . a ring.
Je voudrais . . .	. . . une montre.	. . . une bague.
zhuh voo-dray . . .	. . . *ůne mohntr'.*	. . . *ůne bahg.*

. . . a necklace.	. . . a bracelet.	. . . earrings.
. . . un collier.	. . . un bracelet.	. . . des boucles d'oreille.
. . . *un kohl-yay.*	. . . *un brass-lay.*	. . . *day bookl' doh-ray.*

Is this gold?	. . . platinum?	. . . silver?
Est-ce de l'or?	. . . du platine?	. . . de l'argent?
ess duh lor?	. . . *dů pla-teen?*	. . . *duh lar-zhahn?*

Is it solid or plated?	a diamond
C'est massif ou plaqué?	un diamant
say mà-seef oo pla-kay?	*un dee-ah-mahn*

a pearl	a ruby	a sapphire
une perle	un rubis	un saphir
ůne pairl	*un rů-bee*	*un sa-feer*

an amethyst	a topaz
une améthyste	une topaz
ůne ah-may-teest	*ůne toh-paz*

Antiques

What period is this?	It's beautiful.
C'est de quelle époque?	C'est beau.
say duh kell ay-pohk?	*say bo.*

But very expensive.
Mais très cher.
may tray shair.

How much (is) . . .
Combien (est) . . .
kohn-b'yen (ay) . . .

. . . this book?
. . . ce livre?
. . . suh leevr'?

. . . this picture?
. . . ce tableau?
. . . suh ta-blo?

. . . this map?
. . . cette carte?
. . . set kart?

. . . this frame?
. . . ce cadre?
. . . suh kahdr'?

. . . this piece of furniture?
. . . ce meuble?
. . . suh muhbl'?

Is it an antique?
Est-ce que c'est d'époque?
ess kuh say day-pohk?

Can you ship it?
Pouvez-vous l'expédier?
poo-vay-voo lex-paid-yay?

To this address.
A cette adresse.
ah set ah-dress.

---

1. *Pronounce ů like *ee* with your lips in a tight circle.
2. *zh* is like the *s* in measure.
3. *n* means a nasal "n," pronounced through the nose.

17. Telephone

Talking on the telephone is an excellent test of your ability to communicate in French, because you can't see the person you are talking to or use gestures to help get across your meaning. When asking for someone, simply say his name and add **S'il vous plaît.** If you say the number instead of dialing, give it in pairs. For Passy 6066, you would say 60–66: soixante–soixante-six.

Where is the telephone?
Où est le téléphone?
oo ay luh tay-lay-fohn?

Hello!
Allô!
ah-lo!

The telephone operator
La téléphoniste
la tay-lay-fo-neest

Operator!
Mademoiselle!
mahd-mwa-zell!

Information
Les renseignements
lay rahn-sayn-mahn

The telephone number
of _____ .
Le numéro de téléphone
de _____ .
*luh nǔ-may-ro duh
tay-lay-fohn duh* _____ .

Long distance
Interurbain
en-tair-ǔr-ben

Get me, please, number _____ .
Donnez-moi, s'il vous plaît, le numéro _____ .
do-nay-mwa, seel voo play, luh nǔ-may-ro _____ .

---

1. *Pronounce ǔ like ee with your lips in a tight circle.*
2. *zh is like the s in measure.*
3. *n means a nasal "n," pronounced through the nose.*

Operator, that was the wrong number.
Mademoiselle, c'était le mauvais numéro.
mahd-mwa-zell, say-tay luh mo-vay nŭ-may-ro.

I want to call Washington, in the United States.
Je veux appeler Washington, aux États-Unis.
zhuh vuh zahp-lay washington, oh zay-ta-zŭ-nee.

The number I am calling is _____ .
Le numéro que je demande est _____ .
luh nŭ-may-ro kuh zhuh duh-mahnd ay _____ .

Extension _____ .	**Must I wait long?**
Poste _____ .	Faut-il attendre longtemps?
post _____ .	*fo-teel ah-tahndr' lohn-tahn?*

How much is it per minute?	**My number is _____ .**
C'est combien la minute?	Mon numéro est _____ .
say kohn-b'yen la mee-nŭt?	*mohn nŭ-may-ro*
	ay _____ .

Mr. Simon, please.
Monsieur Simon, s'il vous plaît.
muss-yuh see-mohn, seel voo play.

What?	**Hold the line!**	**He isn't here.**
Comment?	Ne quittez pas!	Il n'est pas là.
ko-mahn?	*nuh kee-tay pas!*	*eel nay pa la.*

When is he coming back?	**When is she coming back?**
Quand revient-il?	Quand revient-elle?
kahn ruhv-yen teel?	*kahn ruhv-yen tell?*

Very well. I'll call back.
Bien. Je rappelerai.
b'yen. zhuh ra-pel-ray.

Can you take a message?
Pouvez-vous prendre un
   message?
*poo-vay voo prahɴdr
   uɴ may-sazh?*

Ask him (her) to call me.
Demandez-lui de m'appeler.
*duh-mahɴ-day-lwee duh
   mahp-lay.*

At this number: _____ .
A ce numéro: _____ .
ah suh nŭ-may-ro: _____

Who is speaking?
Qui est à l'appareil?
Kee ay ta la-pa-ray?

This is Mr. Smith calling.
De la part de Monsieur Smith.
duh lah par duh muss-yuh smith.

That is written S-M-I-T-H.
Cela s'écrit S-M-I-T-H.
suh-la say-kree ess-em-ee-tay-ahsh.

A	B	C	D	E	F	G	H
ah	*bay*	*say*	*day*	*uh*	*ef*	*zhay*	*ahsh*

I	J	K	L	M	N	O	P
ee	*zhee*	*kah*	*el*	*em*	*en*	*oh*	*pay*

Q	R	S	T	U	V	W
kŭ	*air*	*ess*	*tay*	*ŭ*	*vay*	*doo-bl' vay*

X	Y	Z
eeks	*ee grek*	*zed*

En passant: As American and English names are often strange to French ears, you will find the French alphabet very useful for spelling your name when you leave a message.

---

1. *Pronounce* ŭ like *ee* with your lips in a tight circle.
2. *zh* is like the *s* in measure.
3. ɴ means a nasal "n," pronounced through the nose.

Where is a public telephone?
Où y a-t-il un téléphone public?
oo ee ya teel un tay-lay-fohn pů-bleek?

A token, please.
Un jeton, s'il vous plaît.
*un zhuh-tohn, seel voo
  play.*

Another token.
Encore un jeton.
ahn-kohr un zhuh-tohn.

Two twenty-centime pieces.
Deux pièces de vingt centimes.
duh p'yes duh ven sahn-teem.

The telephone book.
L'annuaire téléphonique.
la-nů-air tay-lay-fo-neek.

If there is no public telephone:

May I use your phone?
Je peux me servir de votre téléphone?
zhuh puh muh sair-veer duh votr' tay-lay-fohn?

Go right ahead.
Je vous en prie.
zuh voo zahn pree.

How much do I owe you?
Qu'est-ce que je vous dois?
kess-kuh zhuh voo dwa?

Nothing. It's complimentary.
Rien. C'est gratuit.
r'yen. say gra-twee.

18. Post Office and Telegrams

One of the first things you do when abroad is to write post-cards—**des cartes postales**—to friends and relatives. Here are the words you will need to know in order to mail them. You might also impress your friends by writing a few words in French, which you will find at the end of this section.

Where is the post office?
Où est le Bureau de Postes?
oo ay luh bŭ-ro duh post?

Where is the mailbox?
Où est la boîte à lettres?
oo ay la bwaht ah let-tr'?

How much do I put on?
Combien faut-il mettre?
kohn-b'yen fo-teel met-tr'?

. . . for letters.
. . . pour des lettres.
. . . poor day lettr'.

Airmail to Canada.
Par avion au Canada.
par ahv-yohn oh ka-na-da.

. . . to the United States.
. . . aux Etats-Unis.
. . . oh zay-ta-zŭ-nee

. . . to England.
. . . en Angleterre.
. . . ahn ahn-gluh-tair.

. . . to Australia.
. . . en Australie.
. . . ahn ohss-tra-lee.

How much is it . . . ?
C'est combien . . . ?
say kohn-b'yen . . . ?

. . . for postcards?
. . . pour cartes postales?
. . . poor kart pohs-tahl?

For names of other countries, see dictionary.

Registered.
Recommendé.
ruh-ko-mahn-day.

Insured.
Assuré.
ah-sŭ-ray.

---

1. Pronounce *ŭ* like *ee* with your lips in a tight circle.
2. *zh* is like the *s* in measure.
3. *n* means a nasal "n," pronounced through the nose.

Where can I send a telegram?
Où est-ce que je peux télégraphier?
oo ess kuh zhuh puh tay-lay-graf-yay?

How much is it per word?
C'est combien le mot?
say kohn-b'yen luh mo?

I need . . . writing paper.
J'ai besoin . . .
  de papier à lettres.
zhay buh-zwen . . .
  duh pap-yay ah lettr'.

. . . envelopes.
. . . d'enveloppes.
. . . dahn-vuh-lohp.

Can you lend me . . .
Pouvez-vous me prêter . . .
poo-vay-voo muh pray-tay . . .

. . . a pen?
. . . un stylo?
. . . un stee-lo?

. . . some stamps?
. . . des timbres?
. . . day ten-br'?

. . . a pencil?
. . . un crayon?
. . . un kray-yohn?

Dear John,
Mon cher Jean,
mohn shair zhahn,

Dear Jane,
Ma chère Jeanne,
ma shair zhahn,

I miss you.
Vous me manquez.
voo muh mahn-kay.

Best regards from Nice.
Bons souvenirs de Nice.
bohn soov-neer duh neece.

Best wishes to everyone.
Amitiés à tout le monde.
ah-meet-yay ah tool-mohnd.

All the best.
Bien à vous.
b'yen nah voo.

19. Seasons and the Weather

winter	spring	summer	autumn
l'hiver	le printemps	l'été	l'automne
lee-vair	*luh pren-tahn*	*lay-tay*	*lo-tohn*

How is the weather?
Quel temps fait-il?
kel tahn fay-teel?

The weather is fine.
Il fait beau.
eel fay bo.

Let's go swimming.
Allons nager.
ah-lohn na-zhay.

Where is the pool?
Où est la piscine?
oo ay la pee-seen?

It's very hot.
Il fait très chaud.
eel fay tray sho.

It's cold.
Il fait froid.
eel fay frwah.

It's raining.
Il pleut.
eel pluh.

I need . . . an umbrella.
J'ai besoin . . . d'un parapluie.
zhay buh-zwen . . . dun pa-ra-plwee.

. . . boots.
. . . de bottes.
. . . duh boht.

. . . a raincoat.
. . . d'un imperméable.
. . . dun nen-pair-may-abl'.

What a fog!
Quel brouillard!
kel broo-yahr!

One can't see anything.
On n'y voit rien.
on nee vwa r'yen.

It's snowing.
Il neige.
eel nayzh.

Do you like to ski?
Aimez-vous faire du ski?
ay-may-voo fair dǔ ski?

---

1. *Pronounce ǔ like ee with your lips in a tight circle.
2. *zh* is like the *s* in measure.
3. *n* means a nasal "n," pronounced through the nose.

I want to rent skis.
Je voudrais louer des skis.
zhuh voo-dray loo-ay day skee.

Where's the tow?
Où est le remonte-pente?
oo ay luh ruh-mohnt-pahnt?

Where is the beach?
Où est la plage?
oo ay la plazh?

I want to rent . . .
Je voudrais louer . . .
zhah voo-dray loo-ay . . .

. . . a boat.
. . . un bateau.
. . . un ba-toh.

. . . a mask and fins.
. . . une masque et des palmes.
. . . une mahsk' ay day palm.

. . . air tanks.
. . . des bouteilles d'air.
. . . day boo-tay dair.

Can one dive here?
Peut-on plonger ici?
puh-tohn plohn-zhay ee-see?

Are there sharks?
Y a-t-il des requins?
ee-ya-teel day ruh-kan?

En passant: Temperature is expressed in Centigrade, not Fahrenheit. Zero is freezing in Centigrade, and 100° is boiling. To change Centigrade to Fahrenheit, multiply by 9/5 and add 32°. To change Fahrenheit to Centigrade, subtract 32° and multiply by 5/9.

DOCTOR

I am ill.
Je suis malade.
zhuh swee ma-lahd.

My wife is sick.
Ma femme est malade.
ma fahm ay ma-lahd.

My husband is ill.
Mon mari est malade.
mohn ma-ree ay ma-lahd.

My child is ill.
Mon enfant est malade.
mohn nahn fahn ay ma-lahd.

My friend is ill.
Mon ami est malade.
mohn na-mee ay ma-lahd.

I need a doctor.
J'ai besoin d'un médecin.
zhay buh-zwen d'un maid-sen.

When can he come here?
Quand peut-il venir?
kahn puh-teel vuh-neer?

Well, what's wrong with you?
Bien, qu'est-ce que vous avez?
b'yen, kess kuh voo za-vay?

I don't feel well.
Je ne me sens pas bien.
zhuh nuh muh sahn pa b'yen.

Where does it hurt?
Où avez-vous mal?
oo ah-vay-voo mahl?

Here.
Ici.
ee-see.

---

1. *Pronounce* ů *like* ee *with your lips in a tight circle.*
2. *zh is like the s in measure.*
3. *n means a nasal "n," pronounced through the nose.*

125

I have a pain . . .	. . . in my head.	. . . in the throat.
J'ai mal . . .	. . . à la tête.	. . . à la gorge.
zhay mahl . . .	*. . . ah la tet.*	*. . . ah la gorzh.*

. . . in the ear.	. . . in the stomach.	. . . in the back.
. . . à l'oreille.	. . . à l'estomac.	. . . au dos.
. . . ah lohr-ay.	*. . . ah lay-sto-ma.*	*. . . oh doh.*

I hurt . . .	. . . my leg.	. . . my foot.
Je me suis fait mal . . .	. . . à la jambe.	. . . au pied.
zhuh muh swee fay mahl . . .	*. . . ah la zhahnb'.*	*. . . oh p'yay.*

. . . my arm.	. . . my ankle.	. . . my hand.
. . . au bras.	. . . à la cheville.	. . . à la main.
. . . oh bra.	*. . . ah la shuh-vee.*	*. . . ah la men.*

I am dizzy.
J'ai le vertige.
zhay luh vair-teezh.

I have fever.
J'ai de la fièvre.
zhay duh la f'yevr'.

I can't sleep.
Je ne peux pas dormir.
zhuh nuh puh pa dohr-meer.

I have diarrhea.
J'ai la diarrhée.
zhay la d'ya-ray.

Since when?
Depuis quand?
duh-pwee kahn?

Since yesterday.
Depuis hier.
duh-pwee ee-yair.

Since two days ago.
Depuis deux jours.
duh-pwee duh zhoor.

What have you eaten?
Qu'est-ce que vous avez mangé?
kess kuh voo za-vay mahn-zhay?

Undress.
Déshabillez-vous.
day-za-bee-yay voo.

Lie down.
Couchez-vous.
koo-shay-voo.

Sit up.
Redressez-vous.
ruh-dray-say-voo.

Breathe deeply.
Respirez profondément.
ress-pee-ray pro-fohn-day-mahn.

Open your mouth.
Ouvrez la bouche.
oo-vray la boosh.

Show me your tongue.
Tirez la langue.
tee-ray la lahng.

Cough.
Toussez.
too-say.

Get dressed again.
Rhabillez-vous.
ra-bee-yay-voo.

It is necessary to . . .
Il faut . . .
eel fo . . .

. . . stay in bed.
. . . rester au lit.
. . . ress-tay oh lee.

. . . go to the hospital.
. . . aller à l'hôpital.
. . . tah-lay ah lo-pee-tahl.

. . . take these pills.
. . . prendre cès pilules.
. . . prahndr' say pee-lůl'.

. . . take this prescription.
. . . suivre cette ordon-
nance.
. . . sweevr' set ohr-doh-nahnss.

Is it serious?
C'est grave?
say grahv?

Don't worry.
Ne vous en faites pas.
nuh voo zahn fett pa.

It's not serious.
Ce n'est pas grave.
suh nay pa grahv.

You have . . .
Vous avez . . .
voo za-vay . . .

. . . indigestion.
. . . une indigestion.
. . . ůne en-dee-zhest-yohn.

---

1. *Pronounce ů like ee* with your lips in a tight circle.
2. *zh* is like the *s* in measure.
3. *n* means a nasal "n," pronounced through the nose.

. . . an infection.
. . . une infection.
. . . *ûne en-fex-yohn.*

. . . a cold.
. . . un rhume.
. . . *un rûme.*

. . . a heart attack.
. . . une crise cardiaque.
. . . *ûne kreez kard-yahk.*

. . . appendicitis.
. . . une appendicite.
. . . *ûne ah-pahn-dee-seet.*

. . . liver trouble
. . . une crise de foie.
. . . *ûne kreez duh fwa.*

Be careful.
Attention.
ah-tahns-yohn.

Don't eat too much.
Ne mangez pas trop.
nuh mahn-zhay pa tro.

Don't drink any alcohol.
Ne buvez pas d'alcool.
nuh bû-vay pa dahl-kohl.

Except wine, naturally.
Sauf du vin, naturellement.
*sohf dû van, na-tûr-rel-
mahn.*

How is it going today?
Comment ça va aujourd'hui?
ko-mahn sa va oh-zhoor-dwee?

Badly.	**Better.**	**Much better.**
Mal.	Mieux.	Beaucoup mieux.
mahl.	*m'yuh.*	*bo-koo m'yuh.*

En passant: The Centigrade scale is also used to measure body temperature (see p. 124). The normal body temperature is 36.7 degrees. So if you have anything higher than this, you have a fever—**Vous avez de la fièvre.**

DENTIST

In the unlikely event that the dentist should hurt you, tell him "Stop!"—**Arrêtez!**—or "Wait a minute!"—**Attendez une minute!** This will give you time to regain your courage.

Can you recommend a dentist?
Pouvez-vous recommander un dentiste?
poo-vay voo ruh-ko-mahn-day un dahn-teest?

I have a toothache.
J'ai mal aux dents.
zhay mahl oh dahn.

It hurts here.
J'ai mal là.
zhay mahl la.

You need a filling.
Il vous faut un plombage.
eel voo fo tun plohn-bahzh.

There is an infection.
Il y a de l'infection.
eel ee ya duh len-fex-yohn.

The tooth must come out.
Il faut arracher cette dent.
eel fo ta-ra-shay set dahn.

Will it take long?
Est-ce que ce sera long?
ess kuh suh suh-ra lohn?

Just fix it temporarily.
Arrangez-la temporairement.
ah-rahn-zhay-la tahn-po-rair-mahn.

An injection against pain, please.
Une piqûre contre la douleur, s'il vous plaît.
ůne pee-kůr kohn-tr' la doo-lurr, seel voo play.

---

1. *Pronounce ů like ee with your lips in a tight circle.*
2. *zh is like the s in measure.*
3. *n means a nasal "n," pronounced through the nose.*

Does it hurt?
Ça fait mal?
sa fay mahl?

Yes, a little.
Oui, un peu.
wee, un puh.

Not at all.
Pas du tout.
pa dŭ too.

Is it finished?
C'est fini?
say fee-nee?

How much do I owe you?
Combien je vous dois?
kohn-b'yen zhuh voo dwa?

21. Problems and Police

Although the situations suggested below may never happen to you, the words are useful to know, just in case.

Go away!
Allez-vous en!
ah-lay voo zahn!

Leave me alone.
Laissez-moi tranquille.
lay-say mwah trahn-keel.

. . . or I'll call a policeman.
. . . ou j'appelle un agent.
. . . oo zha-pel un na-zhahn.

Help!
Au secours!
o skoor!

Police!
Police!
po-leess!

What's going on?
Qu'est-ce qui se passe?
kess kee suh pahss?

This man is following me.
Cet homme me poursuit.
set ohm muh poor-swee.

Where is the police station?
Où est le commissariat de police?
oo ay luh ko-mee-sahr-ya duh po-leess?

I have been robbed of . . .
On m'a volé . . .
ohn ma vo-lay . . .

. . . my wallet.
. . . mon portefeuille.
. . . mohn port-foy.

I've lost . . .
J'ai perdu . . .
zhay pair-dů . . .

. . . my watch.
. . . ma montre.
. . . ma mohntr'.

. . . my jewelry.
. . . mes bijoux.
. . . may bee-zhoo.

---

1. *Pronounce ů like ee with your lips in a tight circle.*
2. *zh is like the s in measure.*
3. *n means a nasal "n," pronounced through the nose.*

. . . **my suitcase**
. . . ma valise
. . . *ma va-leez*

. . . **my traveler's checks**
. . . mes chèques de voyage
. . . *may shek duh vwa-yahzh*

. . . **my passport.**
. . . mon passeport.
. . . *mohn pass-pohr.*

Stop, thief!
Au voleur!
oh vo-lurr!

Stop that man!
Arrêtez cet homme!
ah-ray-tay set ohm!

That's the one!
C'est celui-là!
say suh-lwee-la.

I wish to make a complaint.
Je veux porter plainte.
zhuh vuh pohr-tay plant.

Calm down!
Calmez-vous!
kahl-may-voo!

Don't worry.
Ne vous en faites pas.
nuh voo zahn fett pa.

Remain here!
Restez ici!
ress-tay zee-see!

Is this your property?
Est-ce votre propriété?
ess-suh vohtr' pro-pree-ay-tay?

Fill in this form.
Remplissez ce formulaire.
rahn-plee-say suh for-mü-lair.

This man insists that . . .
Cet homme pretend que . . .
sett ohm pray-tahn kuh . . .

It's a misunderstanding.
C'est un malentendu.
say tun ma-lahn-tahn-dü.

Here are your things.
Voici vos affaires.
vwa-see vo zaf-fair.

You can leave.
Vous pouvez partir.
voo poo-vay par-teer.

Thank you!
Merci!
mair-see!

Wait! My passport is missing!
Attendez! C'est mon passeport qui manque.
ah-tahɴ-day! say mohɴ pass-por kee mahɴk.

I want to notify my consulate.
Je voudrais notifier mon consulat.
zhuh voo-dray no-teef-yay mohɴ ҟohɴ-sŭ-la.

---

1. *Pronounce* ŭ *like* ee *with your lips in a tight circle.*
2. *zh* is like the *s* in measure.
3. ɴ means a nasal "n," pronounced through the nose.

22. Housekeeping

The following chapter will be especially interesting for those who stay for a time in France or have occasion to employ French-speaking baby-sitters or household help, abroad or even at home.

What is your name?
Comment vous appelez-vous?
ko-mahn voo zahp-lay-voo?

Where have you worked before?
Où avez-vous travaillé avant?
oo ah-vay-voo tra-va-yay ah-vahn?

Can you take care of a baby?
Savez-vous vous occuper d'un bébé?
sa-vay-voo voo zo-kŭ-pay dun bay-bay?

Do you know how to cook?
Savez-vous faire la cuisine?
sa-vay-voo fair la kwee-zeen?

This is your room.
Voici votre chambre.
vwa-see votr' shahnbr'.

Thursday will be your day off.
Le jeudi sera votre jour de congé.
luh zhuh-dee suh-ra votr' zhoor duh kohn-zhay.

We will pay you _____ per week.
Nous vous paierons _____ par semaine.
noo voo pay-rohn _____ par suh-men.

Please clean . . .
Nettoyez, s'il vous plaît . . .
nay-twa-yay, seel voo play . . .

. . . the living room.
. . . le salon.
. . . luh sa-lohn.

---

1. *Pronounce ŭ* like *ee* with your lips in a tight circle.
2. *zh* is like the *s* in measure.
3. *n* means a nasal "n," pronounced through the nose.

. . . **the dining room.**
. . . la salle à manger.
. . . *la sahl ah mahn-zhay.*

. . . **the bedroom.**
. . . la chambre.
. . . *la shahnbr'.*

. . . **the bathroom.**
. . . la sàlle de bain.
. . . *la sahl duh ben.*

. . . **the kitchen.**
. . . la cuisine.
. . . *la kwee-zeen.*

Wash the dishes.
Faites la vaisselle.
fett la vay-sell.

Sweep the floor.
Balayez le plancher.
ba-lay-yay luh plahn-shay.

Use the vacuum cleaner.
Prenez l'aspirateur.
pruh-nay lahss-pee-ra-terr.

. . . **the broom.**
. . . le balai.
. . . *luh ba-lay.*

Polish the silver.
Faites l'argenterie.
fett lahr-zhahnt-ree.

Have you finished?
Avez-vous fini?
ah-vay voo fee-nee?

Make the beds.
Faites les lits.
fett lay lee.

Change the sheets.
Changez les draps.
shahn-zhay lay dra.

Wash this.
Lavez ceci.
la-vay suh-see.

Use bleach.
Mettez de l'eau de Javel.
may-tay duh lo duh zha-vel.

Iron that.
Repassez cela.
ruh-pa-say suh-la.

Mend this.
Recousez ceci.
ruh-koo-zay suh-see.

What do we need?
De quoi avons-nous besoin?
duh kwa ah-vohn-noo buh-zwen?

Go to the market.
Allez au marché.
ah-lay oh mar-shay.

Here is the list.
Voici la liste.
vwa-see la leest.

Put the milk in the refrigerator.
Mettez le lait au frigidaire.
may-tay luh lay oh free-zhee-dair.

If someone calls, write the name here.
Si quelqu'un appelle, écrivez le nom ici.
see kel-kun ah-pell, ay-kree-vay luh nohn ee-see.

I'll be at this number.
Je serai à ce numéro.
zhuh suh-ray ah suh nŭ-may-ro.

I'll be back at 4 o'clock.
Je serai de retour à quatre heures.
zhuh suh-ray duh ruh-toor ah katr' err.

Give the baby a bottle at _____ o'clock.
Donnez un biberon au bébé à _____ heures.
doh-nay un beeb-rohn oh bay-bay ah _____ err.

Give the child a bath.
Donnez un bain à l'enfant.
doh-nay zun ben ah lahn-fahn.

Put him to bed at _____ o'clock.
Mettez-le au lit à _____ heures.
may-tay-luh oh lee ah _____ err.

Did anyone call?
Est-ce que quelqu'un a téléphoné?
ess-kuh kell-kun ah tay-lay-fo-nay?

Serve lunch at 1 o'clock.
Servez le déjeuner à une heure.
sair-vay luh day-zhuh-nay ah ŭne err.

---

1. *Pronounce ŭ like ee with your lips in a tight circle.*
2. *zh is like the s in measure.*
3. *n means a nasal "n," pronounced through the nose.*

There will be guests this evening.
Il y aura des invités ce soir.
eel ee oh-ra day zen-vee-tay suh swahr.

Set the table for eight places.
Préparez la table pour huit couverts.
pray-pair-ay la tahbl' poor weet coo-vair.

Serve dinner at 9 o'clock.
Servez le dîner à neuf heures.
sair-vay luh dee-nay ah nuh verr.

Arrange these flowers on the table.
Disposez ces fleurs sur la table.
dee-spo-zay say flerr sur la tahbl'.

Someone is ringing the door bell.
On sonne à la porte.
ohn sonn ah la port'.

Open the door, please.
Ouvrez la porte, s'il vous plaît.
oo-vray la port', seel voo play.

23. Some Business Phrases

You will find the short phrases and vocabulary in this section extremely useful if you are on a business trip to France, Canada, Switzerland, Belgium, or to other French-speaking parts of the world. While it is true that English is a prominent foreign language used in the French-speaking world and that efficient interpreters are available, these phrases will add another dimension to your contacts with your French-speaking business associates. The fact that you have made the effort to master some business expressions will be a compliment to your hosts and will indicate that you, by using some phrases in their language, are reciprocating their traditional politeness.

Good morning, Miss.
Bonjour, mademoiselle.
bohn-zhoor mahd-mwa-zell.

Is Mr. Montfort in?
Monsieur Montfort est là?
Muss-yuh mohn-for ay la?

I have an appointment with him.
J'ai rendez-vous avec lui.
zhay rahn-day-voo ah-vek l'wee.

My name is . . .
Je m'appelle . . .
zhuh ma-pell . . .

Here is my card.
Voici ma carte.
vwa-see ma kart.

He is expecting you, sir.
Il vous attend, monsieur.
eel voo za-tahn, muss-yuh.

---

1. *Pronounce ů like ee with your lips in a tight circle.
2. zh is like the s in measure.
3. n means a nasal "n," pronounced through the nose.

This way please.
Par ici, s'il vous plaît.
par ee-see seel voo play.

Welcome to France, Mr. Hall.
Bienvenu en France, Monsieur Hall.
b'yen-vuh-nǔ ahn frahnss, muss-yuh Ahl.

How do you find Paris?
Comment trouvez-vous Paris?
ko-mahn troo-vay-voo pa-ree?

It's a magnificent city!
C'est une ville magnifique!
say tǔne veel mahn-yee-feek!

Thank you for giving me this appointment.
Je vous remercie de m'avoir accordé ce rendez-vous.
zhuh voo ruh-mair-see duh ma-vwar ah-kor-day
suh rahn-day-voo.

According to your letter . . .
Selon votre lettre . . .
suh-lohn votr' lettr' . . .

. . . you are interested in our business machines.
. . . nos machines commerciales vous intéressent.
. . . no ma-sheen ko-mair-s'yahl voo zan-tay-ress.

Here is our most recent catalog.
Voici notre catalogue le plus récent.
vwa-see notr' ka-ta-lohg luh plu ray-sahn.

And these are our new models . . .
Et voici nos nouveaux modèles . . .
ay vwa-see no noo-vo mo-dell . . .

. . . of computers and photo-copiers.
. . . d'ordinateurs et de machines à photo-copier.
. . . dor-dee-na-terr ay duh ma-sheen ah fo-toh-kohp-yay.

Thank you. It looks very interesting.
Merci. Cela semble être très intéressant.
mair-see. Suh-la sahnbl' etr' tray zan-tay-reh-sahn.

Can you come back Wednesday morning?
Pouvez-vous revenir mercredi matin?
poo-vay-voo ruhv-neer mair-kreh-dee ma-ten?

We wish to place an order.
Nous voulons faire une commande.
noo voo-lohn fair ûne ko-mahnd.

We expect a discount of _____ .
Nous espérons une remise de _____ .
noo zess-pay-rohn ûne ruh-meez duh _____ .

What are the terms of payment?
Quelles sont les conditions de paiement?
kell sohn lay kohn-deess-yohn duh pay-mahn?

By bank draft—30-day . . .
Par traite bancaire de trente jours . . .
par trait bahn-kair duh trahnt zhoor . . .

. . . 60 day, 90 day.
. . . soixante jours, quatre-vingt-dix jours.
. . . swa-sahnt zhoor, katr-ven-dee zhoor.

Irrevocable letter of credit.
Lettre de crédit irrévocable.
letr' duh cray-dee eer-ray-vo-kahbl'.

We have an account with the _____ Bank.
Nous avons un compte avec la Banque _____ .
noo za-vohn zun kohnt ah-vek la bahnk _____ :

---

1. *Pronounce* û *like* ee *with your lips in a tight circle.*
2. *zh is like the s in measure.*
3. *n means a nasal "n," pronounced through the nose.*

When can we expect . . .
Quand pouvons nous attendre . . .
kahn poo-vohn noo ah-tahndr' . . .

. . . shipment?
. . . l'expédition?
. . . lex-pay-deess-yohn?

. . . delivery?
. . . la livraison?
. . . la leev-ray-zohn?

Are these your best terms?
Ce sont vos meilleures conditions?
suh sohn vo may-yerr kohn-deess-yohn?

We are in agreement, aren't we?
Nous sommes d'accord, n'est-ce past?
noo somm da-kor, ness-pa?

We need time . . .
Nous avons besoin d'un délai . . .
noo za-vohn buh-zwen d'un day-lay . . .

. . . to study the contract.
. . . pour étudier le contrat.
. . . poor ay-tŭd-yay luh kohn-tra.

Our lawyers will contact you.
Nos avocats vous contacteront.
No za-vo-ka voo kohn-tahk-tuh-rohn.

It's a pleasure . . .
C'est un plaisir . . .
say tun play-zeer . . .

. . . to do business with you.
. . . de faire des affaires avec vous.
. . . duh fair day zah-fair ah-vek voo.

We would like to invite you to dinner.
Nous voudrions vous inviter à diner.
Noo voo-dree-yohn voo zen-vee-tay ah dee-nay.

We will call for you . . .
Nous viendrons vous chercher . . .
noo v'yen-drohn voo shair-shay . . .

. . . at the hotel at 8 o'clock.
. . . à l'hôtel à 8 heures.
. . . ah lo-tel ah weet err.

You are very kind.
Vous êtes tres aimable.
voo zett tray zay-mahbl'.

Thank you for the excellent dinner.
Merci pour l'excellent dîner.
mair-see poor lex-sel-lahn dee-nay.

It was a pleasure to meet you.
C'était un plaisir de faire votre connaissance.
say-tay tun play-zeer duh fair votr' ko-nay-sahnss.

If you visit America don't fail . . .
Si vous visitez l'Amérique ne manquez pas . . .
see voo vee-zee-tay la-may-reek nuh mahn-kay pa . . .

. . . to let us know.
. . . de nous prévenir.
. . . duh noo pray-vuh-neer.

---

1. *Pronounce ǔ* like *ee* with your lips in a tight circle.
2. *zh* is like the *s* in measure.
3. *n* means a nasal "n," pronounced through the nose.

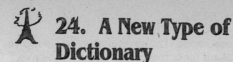

24. A New Type of Dictionary

The following dictionary supplies a list of English words and their translation into French, which will enable you to make up your own sentences in addition to those given in the phrase book. By using these words in conjunction with the following advice and shortcuts, you will be able to make up hundreds of sentences by yourself. Only one French equivalent is given for each English word—the one most useful to you—so you won't be in any doubt regarding which word to use. Every word in this dictionary is followed by the phonetic pronunciation, so you will have no difficulty being understood.

All French nouns are either masculine or feminine, and the adjective that goes with the noun (usually following it) must be masculine or feminine as well. In this dictionary (m) denotes a masculine noun and (f) a feminine one. The feminine of adjectives is usually formed by adding an *e:*

the green suit   **le costume vert**
   (**Le** is the masculine form of "the.")
the green dress   **la robe verte**
   (**La** is the feminine form of "the.")
   (**Le** or **la** becomes **l'** before a noun starting with a vowel.)

When two forms are given in the dictionary for an adjective, the first is masculine and the second is feminine.

Plurals are generally formed by adding **s**, or sometimes **x**. When the plural ends in **x**, this will be indicated in the dictionary.

the green dresses   **les robes vertes**
   (**Les** is the plural form of "the" for both masculine and feminine.)

French verbs change their forms according to the person or object performing the action. The most important forms you will need for each verb are given within the different sections of the phrase book. To help you make up your own sentences, the present tense forms for "to be," "to have," "to come," "to go," and "to want" are given in the dictionary.

The verbs in the dictionary are in the infinitive form and change their ending according to the subject. Although a full grammatical explanation is not within the scope of this book, the following table will help you to use and recognize the important present tense forms of most of the verbs in the dictionary.

Verbs are divided in three groups, according to their infinitive endings: verbs in -er form the first group; those in ir the second; and those in -re and -oir together form the third group. Parler (to speak) and finir (to finish) are examples of the first and second groups; perdre (to lose) and recevoir (to receive) are examples of the third group. Most French verbs belong to the first group. Each verb has six forms in each tense. Here is the present tense of parler (to speak) with its English equivalents:

je parle	I speak *or* I am speaking
tu parles	you speak *or* you are speaking (familiar)
il, elle parle	he, she speaks *or* he, she is speaking
nous parlons	we speak *or* we are speaking.
vous parlez	you speak *or* you are speaking (formal)
ils, elles parlent	they speak *or* they are speaking (masc. or fem.)

We have not indicated a pronoun for "it" because, in French, every noun is either masculine or feminine; therefore, "it" is either "he" or "she."

Tu and vous both mean "you." However, you should use vous, the polite form. Tu, the familiar form, singular only, is used within the family, between close friends, among students, and to children.

The six forms for the present tense of the second and third verb groups are:

finir: je finis, tu finis, il finit, nous finissons, vous finissez, ils finissent

perdre: je perds, tu perds, il perd, nous perdons, vous perdez, ils perdent
recevoir: je reçois, tu reçois, il reçoit, nous recevons, vous recevez, ils reçoivent
(The little hook under the *c* means that it is pronounced like an *s*.)

You can do a lot of communicating by using simply the present tense. But, in addition, you can use the infinitive to express a variety of other concepts. To say something must be done or is necessary, use **il faut** directly with the infinitive (that is, the form given in the dictionary):

I must leave.   **Il faut partir.**

To say you want to do something, use the appropriate form of "want" with the infinitive of the verbs expressing what you want to do:

I want to leave.   **Je veux partir.**

For the negative, put **ne** and **pas** around the verb:

I don't want to leave.   **Je ne veux pas partir.**

An easy way to give a command or make a request is to say, "Do you want . . ." ("Will you . . .")—**Voulez-vous . . .**—followed by an infinitive:

Will you come in?   **Voulez-vous entrer?**

In any case, the imperative is not difficult. It is the same form as that used for "you"—**vous**—but *without* the pronoun:

You are leaving.   **Vous partez.**
Leave!   **Partez!**

An easy way to express what will happen in the future is to use a form of **aller** (to go) with the next verb in the infinitive:

He is going to buy a ticket.   **Il va acheter un billet.**

To form the past tense of the majority of the verbs given in the dictionary, use the present tense of "to have"—**avoir**—with the past participle:

I have been (I was)   **J'ai été**

Since only the most important or irregular past participles are given in the dictionary, note how the past participles are formed for the three groups of French verbs whose infinitives end in **-er, -ir, -re,** or **-oir:**

	"to speak"	"to finish"	"to sell"	"to receive"
infinitive:	**parler**	**finir**	**vendre**	**recevoir**
past participle:	**parlé**	**fini**	**vendu**	**reçu**

To make the past, use of the present of **avoir** with the past participle of the verb you wish to use in the past:

I spoke. (I have spoken.)   **J'ai parlé.**

Some verbs use "to be"—**être**—for the past tense. These are usually the ones that express coming, going, arriving, leaving, etc.:

He has left. (He left.)   **Il est parti.**

The possessive is always expressed by "of"—**de:**

Robert's car   **la voiture de Robert**

Possessive pronouns are listed in the dictionary.
Object pronouns are given in the dictionary. In a sentence the object pronoun is placed before the verb.

I see her.   **Je la vois.**
Do you understand me?   **Me comprenez-vous?**
I speak to him.   **Je lui parle.**
Don't speak to her.   **Ne lui parlez pas.**

French is full of contractions. "To the"—à plus **le, la,** or **les**—becomes **au, à la** and **aux** respectively. "Of the" is **de** plus the definite articles **le, la** and **les** and becomes **du, de la** and **des.** (These combinations can also mean "some.") The ubiquitous little words **y** and **en** substitute for phrases made with **à** and **de; y** stands for **à** plus a noun, and **en** stands for **de** plus a noun.

With this advice and the suggestions given within the dictionary itself, you will be able to make up countless sentences on your own and to converse with anyone you may meet.

There is, of course, much more to French than these few indications we have given you—including the subtleties of the French verb, the use of partitives, pronouns, contractions, the use of prepositions with verbs, and the numerous idioms, sayings, and references that reflect the spirit, wisdom, wit, and history of France. But you can effectively use this selected basic vocabulary as an important step, or even a springboard, to enter the wonderful world that is the French heritage and, by contant practice, absorb and improve your command of this beautiful language. For, as the French say, "Appetite comes with eating." **L'appétit vient en mangeant.** Once you see how easy and how rewarding it is to speak to people in French, you will have the impetus to progress further.

A

a	un, une	*un, une*
(to be) able	pouvoir	*poo-vwahr*
See "can."		
about (concerning)	concernant	*kohn-sair-nahn*
about (approximately)	environ	*ahn-vee-rohn*
above	au-dessus de	*oh-des-sü duh*
accent	accent (m)	*ak-sahn*
(to) accept	accepter	*ak-sep-tay*
accident	accident (m)	*ak-see-dahn*
account	compte (m)	*kohnt*
across	de l'autre côté (de)	*duh lohtr' ko-tay (duh)*
actor	acteur (m)	*ak-terr*
actress	actrice (f)	*ak-treess*
address	adresse (f)	*ah-dress*
adjective	adjectif (m)	*ad-zhek-teef*
admission	entrée (f)	*ahn-tray*
advertisement	annonce (f)	*ah-nohnss*
adverb	adverbe (m)	*ad-vairb*
advice	conseil (m)	*kohn-say'*
(to be) afraid	avoir peur	*ah-vwahr purr*
Africa	Afrique (f)	*ah-freek*
African	africain, -e	*ah-free-ken, -kain*
after	après	*ah-pray*

afternoon	après-midi (m)	*ah-pray-mee-dee*
again	encore	*ahn-kor*
against	contre	*kohntr'*
age	âge (m)	*azh*
agency	agence (f)	*ah-zhahnss*
agent	agent (m)	*ah-zhahn*
ago	il y a	*eel ee ya*
(Use before *time* ago)		
agreed	entendu	*ahn-tahn-dů*
ahead	en avant	*ahn na-vahn*
air	air (m)	*air*
air-conditioned	climatisé, -e	*klee-ma-tee-zay*
(by) air mail	par avion	*par-av-yohn*
airplane	avion (m)	*av-yohn*
airport	aéroport (m)	*ah-ay-ro-por*
all	tout, toute	*too, toot*
That's all!	C'est tout!	*say too!*
all right!	Très bien!	*tray b'yen!*
(to) allow	permettre	*pair-metr'*
almost	presque	*presk'*
alone	seul, -e	*sull*
already	déjà	*day-zha*
also	aussi	*oh-see*
always	toujours	*too-zhoor*
(I) am	je suis	*zhuh swee*
ambulance	ambulance (f)	*ahn-bů-lahnss*
America	Amérique (f)	*ah-may-reek*

American	américain, -e	*ah-may-ree-ken, -kane*
amusing	amusant, -e	*ah-mü-zahn, -zahnt*
and	et	*ay*
angel	ange (m)	*ahnzh*
angry	fâché	*fa-shay*
animal	animal (m)	*ah-nee-mahl*
ankle	cheville (f)	*shuh-vee*
annoying	ennuyeux, -euse	*ahn-nwee-yuh, -yuhz*
another	un autre, une autre	*un nohtr', üne ohtr'*
answer	réponse (f)	*ray-pohnss*
any (adj.)	quelque	*kelk'*
any (pronoun)	en	*ahn*
anyone	quelqu'un, -e	*kel-kun, -kün*
anything	quelque chose	*kel-kuh-shohz*
anywhere	n'importe où	*nen-port-oo*
apartment	appartement (m)	*ah-par-tuh-mahn*
apple	pomme (f)	*pom*
appointment	rendez-vous (m)	*rahn-day-voo*
April	avril (m)	*ah-vreel*
Arab, Arabic	Arabe (m or f)	*ah-rahb*
architecture	architecture (f)	*ar-shee-tek-tür*
are		
you are	vous êtes	*voo zet*
we are	nous sommes	*noo som*
they (m) are	ils sont	*eel sohn*

they (f) are	elles sont	*el sohn*
there are	il y a	*eel ee ya*
arm	bras (m)	*bra*
army	armée (f)	*ar-may*
around here	par ici	*par ee-see*
(to) arrive	arriver	*ah-ree-vay*
art	art (m)	*ahr*
artist	artiste (m or f)	*ar-teest*
as	comme	*kom*
ashtray	cendrier (m)	*sahn-dree-yay*
Asia	Asie	*ah-zee*
(to) ask	demander	*duh-mahn-day*
asleep	endormi, -e	*ahn-dor-mee*
asparagus	asperge (f)	*ass-pairzh*
aspirin	aspirine (f)	*ass-pee-reen*
assortment	assortiment (m)	*ah-sor-tee-mahn*
at	à	*ah*
at the	au (m); à la (f)	
Atlantic	Atlantique (m)	*at-lahn-teek*
atomic	atomique	*ah-to-meek*
attractive	joli, -e	*zho-lee*
August	août	*oo*
aunt	tante (f)	*tahnt*
Australia	Australie (f)	*ohss-tra-lee*
Australian	australien, -ne	*ohss-tral-yen, -yen*
Austria	Autriche (f)	*o-treesh*
author	auteur (m or f)	*o-terr*

automatic	automatique	*o-toh-ma-teek*
automobile	automobile (f)	*o-toh-mo-beel*
autumn	automne (m)	*o-tohn*
available	disponible	*dees-po-neebl'*
aviation	aviation (f)	*av-yas-yohn*
avoid	éviter	*ay-vee-tay*
away	absent, -e	*ab-sahn, -sahnt*

B

baby	bébé (m)	*bay-bay*
bachelor	célibataire (m)	*say-lee-ba-tair*
back (part of body)	dos (m)	*doh*
bacon	bacon (m)	*ba-kohn*
bad	mauvais, -e	*mo-vay, -vaiz*
That's too bad!	C'est dommage!	*say doh-mazh!*
baggage	bagage (m)	*ba-gazh*
banana	banane (f)	*ba-nahn*
bandage	bandage (m)	*bahn-dazh*
bank	banque (f)	*bahnk*
bar	bar (m)	*bar*
barber	coiffeur (m)	*kwa-furr*
basement	sous-sol (m)	*soo-sol*
basket	panier (m)	*pan-yay*
bath	bain (m)	*ben*

bathing suit	maillot de bain (m)	*ma-yo duh ben*
bathroom	salle de bain (f)	*sahl duh ben*
battery	batterie (f)	*baht-ree*
battle	bataille (f)	*ba-tye*
(to) be	être	*etr'*

(See also "am," "is," "are," "was," "were," "been.")

beach	plage (f)	*plazh*
beans	haricots (m. pl.)	*ah-ree-ko*
bear	ours (m)	*oorss*
beard	barbe (f)	*barb*
beautiful	beau, belle	*bo, bel*
beauty	beauté (f)	*bo-tay*
beauty shop	salon de beauté (m)	*sa-lohn duh bo-tay*
because	parce que	*par-suh-kuh*
bed	lit	*lee*
bedroom	chambre (f)	*shahnbr'*
bedspread	dessus de lit (m)	*duh-sŭ duh lee*
beef	boeuf (m)	*buhf*
been	été	*ay-tay*
I have been	j'ai été	*zhay ay-tay*
beer	bière (f)	*b'yair*
before (time)	avant	*ah-vahn*
(to) begin	commencer	*komahn-say*
behind	derrière	*dair-yair*

(to) believe	croire	*krwahr*
belt	ceinture (f)	*sen-tůr*
besides	d'ailleurs	*da-yerr*
best (adv)	le mieux	*luh m'yuh*
(adj)	le meilleur, la meilleure	*luh, la may-yerr*
better	meilleur, -e	*may-yurr*
between	entre	*ahntr'*
bicycle	bicyclette (f)	*bee-see-klett*
big	gros, -se	*gro, grohss*
bill	note (f)	*noht*
bird	oiseau (m)	*wa-zo*
birthday	anniver- saire (m)	*ah-nee-vair-sair*
black	noir, -e	*nwahr*
blond	blond, -e	*blohn, blohnd*
blood	sang (m)	*sahn*
blue	bleu	*bluh*
boat	bateau (m)	*ba-toh*
body	corps (m)	*kor*
book	livre (m)	*leevr'*
bookstore	librairie (f)	*lee-bray-ree*
born	né	*nay*
(to) borrow	emprunter	*ahn-prun-tay*
boss	patron (m)	*pa-trohn*
both	tous les deux, toutes les deux	*too, toot lay duh*

bottle	bouteille (f)	*boo-tay*
bottom	fond (m)	*fohn*
bought	acheté	*ash-tay*
boy	garçon (m)	*gahr-sohn*
brain	cerveau (m)	*sair-vo*
brake	frein (m)	*fren*
brave	brave	*brahv*
bread	pain (m)	*pan*
(to break)	casser	*ka-say*
breakfast	petit déjeuner (m)	*puh-tee day-zhuh-nay*
(to) breathe	respirer	*res-pee-ray*
bridge	pont (m)	*pohn*
briefcase	serviette	*sair-v'yet*
(to) bring	apporter	*ah-por-tay*
Bring me . . .	Apportez-moi . . .	*ah-por-tay-mwa . . .*
broken	cassé	*ka-say*
brother	frère (m)	*frair*
brother-in-law	beau-frère (m)	*bo-frair*
brown	brun, brune	*brun, brune*
brunette	brune (f)	*brune*
(to) build	construire	*kohn-strweer*
building	bâtiment (m)	*ba-tee-mahn*
built	construit	*kohn-strwee*
bureau	bureau (m)	*bu-ro*
bus	autobus (m)	*oh-toh-buss*

bus stop	arrêt de l'auto- bus (m)	*ah-ray duh lo-toh-bŭss*
business	les affaires (f. pl)	*lay za-fair*
busy	très occupé	*tray zo-kŭ-pay*
but	mais	*may*
butter	beurre (m)	*berr*
button	bouton (m)	*boo-tohn*
(to) buy	acheter	*ash-tay*
by	par	*par*

C

cab	taxi (m)	*tak-see*
cabbage	chou (m)	*shoo*
cake	gâteau (m)	*ga-toh*
(to) call	appeler	*ap-lay*
Call me.	Appelez-moi.	*ap-lay-mwa.*
camera	appareil photo- graphique (m)	*ah-pa-ray fo-toh-gra- feek*
movie	caméra (f)	*ka-may-ra*
can (be able)	pouvoir	*poo-vwahr*
I can	je peux	*zhuh puh*
you can	vous pouvez	*voo poo-vay*
he can	il peut	*eel puh*
she can	elle peut	*el puh*
we can	nous pouvons	*noo poo-vohn*
they (m) can	ils peuvent	*eel puhv*

they (f) can	elles peuvent	*el puhv*
Can you?	Pouvez-vous?	*poo-vay-voo?*
I can't.	Je ne peux pas.	*zhuh nuh puh pa.*
can (container)	boîte (f)	*bwaht*
can opener	ouvre-boîte (m)	*oovr'-bwaht*
candy	bonbon (m)	*bohn-bohn*
cap	casquette (f)	*kas-ket*
cape	cape (f)	*kahp*
captain	capitaine	*ka-pee-tain*
car	auto (f)	*oh-toh*
carburetor	carburateur (m)	*kar-bŭ-ra-turr*
card	carte (f)	*kart*
(Be) careful!	Faites attention!	*fet ah-tahns-yohn*
carrot	carotte (f)	*ka-rot*
(to) carry	porter	*por-tay*
Carry this to . . .	Portez cela à . . .	*por-tay suh-la ah . . .*
cashier	caissier (m), -ière (f)	*kays-yay, -yair*
castle	chateau (m)	*sha-toh*
cat	chat (m)	*sha*
cathedral	cathédrale (f)	*ka-tay-drahl*
catholic	catholique	*ka-toh-leek*
cemetery	cimetière (m)	*seem-t'yair*
cent	centime (m)	*sahn-teem*
center	centre (m)	*sahntr'*

century	siècle (m)	*s'yekl'*
certainly	certainement	*sair-tain-mahn*
chair	chaise (f)	*shaiz*
chandelier	lustre (m)	*lŭstr'*
change	de la monnaie (f)	*duh la mo-nay*
(to) change	échanger	*ay-shahn-zhay*
charming	charmant, -e	*shar-mahn, -mahnt*
chauffeur	chauffeur (m)	*sho-furr*
cheap	bon marché	*bohn mar-shay*
check	chèque (m)	*shek*
checkroom	vestiaire (m)	*vest-yair*
cheese	fromage (m)	*fro-mazh*
cherries	cerises (f. pl.)	*suh-reez*
chest (part of the body)	poitrine (f)	*pwa-treen*
chicken	poulet (m)	*poo-lay*
child	enfant (m or f)	*ahn-fahn*
China	Chine (f)	*sheen*
Chinese	chinois (m), -oise (f)	*sheen-wa, -wahz*
chocolate	chocolat (m)	*sho-ko-la*
chop	côtelette (f)	*koht-let*
church	église (f)	*ay-gleez*
cigar	cigare (m)	*see-gar*
cigarette	cigarette (f)	*see-ga-ret*
city	ville (f)	*veel*
(to) clean	nettoyer	*nay-twa-yay*

clear	clair	*klair*
climate	climat (m)	*klee-ma*
close	près	*pray*
(to) close	fermer	*fair-may*
closed	fermé	*fair-may*
clothes	vêtements (m. pl)	*vett-mahn*
coast	côte (f)	*koht*
coat (overcoat)	manteau (m)	*mahn-toh*
(of suit)	veste (f)	*vest*
coffee	café (m)	*ka-fay*
coin	pièce (m)	*p'yess*
cold	froid, -e	*frwa, frwahd*
college	université (f)	*ŭ-nee-vair-see-tay*
colonel	colonel (m)	*ko-lo-nel*
color	couleur (f)	*koo-lerr*
comb	peigne (m)	*pain*
(to) come	venir	*vuh-neer*
I come	je viens	*zhuh v'yen*
you come	vous venez	*voo vuh-nay*
he comes	il vient	*eel v'yen*
she comes	elle vient	*el v'yen*
we come	nous venons	*noo vuh-nohn*
they (m) come	ils viennent	*eel v'yenn*
they (f) come	elles viennent	*el v'yenn*
Come!	Venez!	*vuh-nay!*
Come in!	Entrez!	*ahn-tray!*

(to) come back	revenir	*ruh-vuh-neer*
company	compagnie (f)	*kohn-pah-nyee*
complete	complet, -ète	*kohn-play, -plait*
computer	ordinateur (m)	*or-dee-na-turr*
concert	concert (m)	*kohn-sair*
congratulations	félicitations (f)	*fay-lee-see-tahss-yohn*
(to) continue	continuer	*kohn-tee-nway*
conversation	conversation (f)	*kohn-vair-sas-yohn*
cook	cuisinier (m), -ière (f)	*kwee-zeen-yay, -yair*
(to) cook	faire la cuisine	*fair la kwee-zeen*
cool	frais, fraîche	*fray, fraish*
copy	copie (f)	*ko-pee*
corkscrew	tire-bouchon (m)	*teer-boo-shohn*
corner	coin (m)	*kwen*
correct	exact, -e	*ek-zakt*
(to) cost	coûter	*koo-tay*
cotton	coton (m)	*ko-tohn*
cough	toux (f)	*too*
country	pays (m)	*pay-ee*
cousin	cousin, -e	*koo-zen, -zeen*
cow	vache (f)	*vash*
crab	crabe (m)	*krahb*
crazy	fou, folle	*foo, fol*
cream	crème (f)	*kraym*

(to) cross	traverser	*tra-vair-say*
crossroads	carrefour (m)	*car-foor*
cup	tasse (f)	*tahss*
customs	douane (f)	*doo-ahnn*
(to) cut	couper	*koo-pay*

D

(to) dance	danser	*dahn-say*
dangerous	dangereux, -reuse	*dahn-zhuh-ruh,-rerrz*
dark	sombre	*sohnbr'*
darling	chéri, -e	*shay-ree*
date (of month)	date (f)	*daht*
daughter	fille (f)	*fee*
daughter-in-law	belle-fille (f)	*bell-fee*
day	jour (m)	*zhoor*
dead	mort, -e	*mor, mort*
dear	cher, chère	*shair*
December	décembre (m)	*day-sahnbr'*
(to) decide	décider	*day-see-day*
deep	profond, -e	*pro-fohn, -fohnd*
delay	retard (m)	*ruh-tar*
delighted	enchanté, -e	*ahn-shahn-tay*
delicious	délicieux, -ieuse	*day-lees-yuh, -yuhz*
dentist	dentiste (m)	*dahn-teest*

department store	grand magasin (m)	*grahи ma-ga-zeи*
desk	bureau (m)	*bй-ro*
detour	détour (m)	*day-toor*
devil	diable (m)	*d'yahbl'*
dictionary	dictionnaire (m)	*deeks-yo-nair*
different	different, -e	*dee-fay-rahи, rahиt*
difficult	difficile	*dee-fee-seel*
(to) dine	dîner	*dee-nay*
dining room	salle à manger (f)	*sahl-ah-mahи-zhay*
dinner	dîner (m)	*dee-nay*
direction	direction (f)	*dee-reks-yohи*
dirty	sale	*sahl*
disappointed	déçu, -e	*day-sй*
discount	réduction	*ray-dйks-yohи*
divorced	divorcé, -e	*dee-vor-say*
dizziness	vertige (m)	*vair-teezh*
(to) do	faire	*fair*

"Do" is not used as an auxiliary for asking questions or for the negative. To ask questions simply put the subject after the verb, or use *Est-ce que*. "Do you want . . ." is *Voulez-vous . . .* or *Est-ce que vous voulez. . . .* For negatives, use *ne* and *pas* around the verb. "I don't want" is *Je ne veux pas*.

Don't do that!	Ne faites pas cela!	*nuh fet pah suh-la!*
dock	quai (m)	*kay*
doctor	docteur (m)	*dohk-terr*

dog	chien	sh'ye*n*
dollar	dollar (m)	doh-lahr
door	porte (f)	port
down, down-stairs	en bas	ah*n* ba
downtown	en ville	ah*n* veel
dress	robe (f)	rohb
(to) drink	boire	bwahr
(to) drive	conduire	koh*n*-dweer
driver	conducteur (m)	koh*n*-dŭk-terr
driver's license	permis de conduire (m)	pair-me duh koh*n*-dweer
drum	tambour (m)	tah*n*-boor
drunk	ivre	eevr'
dry cleaner	teinturier (m)	te*n*-tur-yay
duck	canard (m)	ka-nahr

E

each	chaque	shahk
ear	oreille (f)	oh-ray
early	de bonne heure	duh bunn err
(to) earn	gagner	gahn-yay
earth	terre (f)	tair
east	est (m)	est
easy	facile	fa-seel
(to) eat	manger	mah*n*-zhay

eggs	des oeufs (m. pl)	*day zuh*
eight	huit	*weet*
eighteen	dix-huit	*dee-zweet*
eighty	quatre-vingts	*katr-ven*
either one	n'importe lequel	*nen-port luh-kel*
elbow	coude (m)	*kood*
electricity	électricité (f)	*ay-lek-tree-see-tay*
elephant	éléphant (m)	*ay-lay-fahn*
elevator	ascenseur (m)	*ah-sahn-serr*
else	autre	*ohtr'*
embassy	ambassade (f)	*ahn-ba-sahd*
emergency	urgence (f)	*ŭr-zhahnss*
employee	employé (m)	*ahn-plwa-yay*
end	fin (f)	*fen*
(to) end	finir	*fee-neer*
England	Angleterre	*ahn-gluh-tair*
English	anglais, -e	*ahn-glay, -glaiz*
entertaining	amusant, -e	*a-mŭ-zahn, -zahnt*
error	erreur (f)	*ay-rurr*
European	européen, -enne	*uh-ro-pay-en, -en*
even	même	*mem*
evening	soir (m)	*swahr*
ever	jamais	*zha-may*
every	chaque	*shahk*
everybody	tout le monde	*tool-mohnd*

everything	tout	*too*
exactly	exactement	*ek-zak-tuh-mahn*
excellent	excellent, -lente	*ek-say-lahn, -lahnt*
except	sauf	*sohf*
(to) exchange	échanger	*ay-shahn-zhay*
Excuse me!	Excusez-moil	*ex-kü-zay-mwa!*
exit	sortie (f)	*sor-tee*
expensive	cher, chère	*shair*
experience	expérience (f)	*ex-pair-yahns*
explanation	explication (f)	*ex-plee-kass-yohn*
(to) export	exporter	*ex-por-tay*
extra	extra	*ex-tra*
eye	oeil (m)	*oy*
eyes	yeux	*yuh*

F

face	visage (m)	*vee-zahzh*
factory	usine (f)	*ü-zeen*
fall	chute (f)	*shüte*
(to) fall	tomber	*tohn-bay*
family	famille (f)	*fa-mee*
famous	fameux, -euse	*fa-muh, -muhz*
far	loin	*lwen*
How far?	A quelle distance?	*ah kel dees-tahnss?*
fare	prix (m)	*pree*

farm	ferme (f)	*fairm*
farther	plus loin	*plü lwen*
fast	vite	*veet*
fat	gros, grosse	*gro, grohss*
father	père (m)	*pair*
February	février (m)	*fay-vree-ay*
(to) feel	(se) sentir	*(suh) sahn-teer*
How do you feel?	Comment vous sentez-vous?	*ko-mahn voo sahn-tay-voo?*
fever	fièvre (f)	*f'yevr'*
(a) few	quelques	*kel-kuh*
fifteen	quinze	*kenz*
fifty	cinquante	*senk-ahnt*
(to) fight	se battre	*suh batr'*
(to) fill	remplir	*rahn-pleer*
film	film (m)	*feelm*
finally	enfin	*ahn-fen*
(to) find	trouver	*troo-vay*
finger	doigt (m)	*dwa*
(to) finish	finir	*fee-neer*
finished	fini, -e	*fee-nee*
fire	feu (m)	*fuh*
first	premier, -ère	*pruh-m'yay, -m'yair*
fish	poisson (m)	*pwa-sohn*
(to) fish	pêcher	*pay-shay*
five	cinq	*senk*
flight	vol (m)	*vohl*

floor	plancher (m)	*plahn-shay*
flower	fleur (f)	*flurr*
(to) fly	voler	*vo-lay*
fly (insect)	mouche (f)	*moosh*
food	alimentation (f)	*ah-lee-mahn-tahs-yohn*
foot	pied (m)	*p'yay*
for	pour	*poor*
foreigner	étranger (m), -gère	*ay-trahn-zhay, -zhair*
forest	forêt (f)	*fo-ray*
(to) forget	oublier	*oo-blee-ay*
Don't forget!	N'oubliez pas!	*noo-blee-ay pa!*
fork	fourchette (f)	*foor-shet*
forty	quarante	*ka-rahnt*
fountain	fontaine (f)	*fohn-taine*
four	quatre	*kahtr'*
fourteen	quatorze	*ka-torz*
fox	renard (m)	*ruh-nahr*
France	France (f)	*frahnss*
free	libre	*leebr'*
French	français, -çaise	*frahn-say, -saiz*
fresh	frais, fraîche	*fray, fraish*
Friday	vendredi	*vahn-druh-dee*
fried	frit, frite	*free, freet*
friend	ami (m), -e (f)	*ah-mee*
frog	grenouille (f)	*gruh-nwee*

from	de	*duh*
(in) front (of)	en face de	*ahn fahss duh*
fruit	fruit (m)	*frwee*
full	complet, -plète	*kohn-play, -plett*
funny	drôle	*drohl*
furniture	meubles (m)	*muhbl'*
future	futur (m)	*fü-tür*

G

game	jeu (m)	*zhuh*
garden	jardin (m)	*zhahr-den*
gasoline	essence (f)	*ay-sahnss*
gas station	poste d'essence (m)	*post day-sahnss*
garage	garage (m)	*ga-razh*
general	général	*zhay-nay-rahl*
gentleman	monsieur (m)	*muss-yuh*
German	allemand, -e	*ahl-mahn, -mahnd*
Germany	Allemagne	*ahl-mine*
(to) get (obtain)	obtenir	*ob-tuh-neer*
(to) get (become)	devenir	*duh-vuh-neer*
(to) get off	descendre	*day-sahndr'*
(to) get on	monter	*mohn-tay*
(to) get out	sortir	*sor-teer*
Get out!	Sortez!	*sor-tay!*

gift	cadeau (m)	*ka-doh*
(to) give	donner	*doh-nay*
Give me . . .	Donnez-moi . . .	*doh-nay-mwa*
girl	fille (f)	*fee*
glass	verre (m)	*vair*
glasses	lunettes (f. pl)	*lû-net*
glove	gant (m)	*gahn*
(to) go	aller	*ah-lay*
I go	je vais	*zhuh vay*
you go	vous allez	*voo za-lay*
he goes	il va	*eel va*
she goes	elle va	*el va*
we go	nous allons	*noo za-lohn*
they (m) go	ils vont	*eel vohn*
they (f) go	elles vont	*el vohn*
(to) go away	s'en aller	*sahn na-lay*
Go away!	Allez-vous en!	*ah-lay-voo zahn!*
(to) go back	revenir	*ruh-vuh-neer*
(to) go on	continuer	*kohn-tee-nway*
Go on!	Continuez!	*kohn-tee-nway!*
goat	chèvre (f)	*shevr'*
God	Dieu (m)	*d'yuh*
gold	or (m)	*or*
golf	golf (m)	*gohlf*
good	bon, bonne	*bohn, bunn*
good-bye	au revoir	*ohr-vwahr*

government	gouvernement (m)	*goo-vair-nuh-mahn*
grandfather	grand-père (m)	*grahn-pair*
grandmother	grand-mère (f)	*grahn-mair*
grapes	raisins (m. pl)	*ray-zen*
grateful	reconnaissant, -e	*ruh-ko-nay-sahn, -sahnt*
gray	gris, grise	*gree, greez*
Great!	Formidable!	*for-mee-dahbl'!*
a great many	beaucoup de	*bo-koo-duh*
Greece	Grèce (f)	*gress*
Greek	grec, grecque	*grek*
green	vert, verte	*vair, vairt*
group	groupe (m)	*groop*
guide	guide (m)	*gheed*
guitar	guitare (f)	*ghee-tar*

H

had (past participle)	eu	*ů*
I had	j'ai eu	*zhay ů*
you had	vous avez eu	*voo za-vay zů*
hair	cheveux (m. pl.)	*shuh-vuh*
hairbrush	brosse à cheveux (f)	*brohss ah shuh-vuh*
haircut	coupe de cheveux (f)	*koop duh shuh-vuh*

half	demi, -e	*duh-mee*
hand	main (f)	*men*
happy	heureux, -reuse	*err-ruh, -ruhz*
hard	dur, -e	*důr*
hat	chapeau (m)	*sha-po*
(to) have	avoir	*ah-vwahr*
I have	j'ai	*zhay*
you have	vous avez	*voo za-vay*
he has	il a	*eel ah*
she has	elle a	*el ah*
we have	nous avons	*noo za-vohn*
they (m) have	ils ont	*eel zohn*
they (f) have	elles ont	*el zohn*
Have you?	Avez-vous?	*ah-vay-voo?*
he	il	*eel*
head	tête (f)	*tet*
heart	coeur (m)	*kerr*
heavy	lourd, lourde	*loor, loord*
(to) hear	entendre	*ahn-tahndr'*
Hello!	Allô!	*ah-lo!*
(to) help	aider	*ay-day*
Help!	Au secours!	*oh suh-koor!*
her (dir. object)	la	*la*
(to) her	lui	*lwee*
her (possessive adj.)	son, sa, ses	*sohn, sa, say*
hers (pronoun)	le sien, la sienne	*luh s'yen, la s'yenn*

	les siens,
	  les siennes
		lay s'yen,
		  lay s'yenn

here	ici	*ee-see*
high	haut, -e	*oh, oht*
highway	route (f)	*root*
hill	colline (f)	*ko-leen*
him	le	*luh*
(to) him	lui	*lwee*
his (adj.)	son, sa, ses	*sohn, sa, say*

his (pronoun)	le sien,
	  la sienne
	les siens,
	  les siennes
		luh s'yen,
		  la s'yenn
		lay s'yen,
		  lay s'yenn

history	histoire (f)	*ees-twahr*
home		
(at my) home	chez moi	*shay mwa*
(at) home	à la maison	*ah la may-zohn*
horse	cheval (m)	*shuh-vahl*
hospital	hôpital (m)	*oh-pee-tahl*
hot	chaud, -e	*sho, shohd*
hotel	hôtel (m)	*o-tel*
hour	heure (f)	*err*
house	maison (f)	*may-zohn*
how	comment	*ko-mahn*
however	pourtant	*poor-tahn*
hundred	cent (m)	*sahn*
(to be) hungry	avoir faim	*ah-vwarh fen*
(to be in a) hurry	être pressé	*etr' pray-say*

Hurry up!	Dépêchez-vous!	*day-pay-shay-voo!*
husband	mari (m)	*ma-ree*

I

I	je	*zhuh*
ice	glace (f)	*glahss*
ice cream	glace (f)	*glahss*
idea	idée (f)	*ee-day*
idiot	idiot (m), idiote (f)	*eed-yo, -yot*
if	si	*see*
ill	malade	*ma-lahd*
(to) import	importer	*en-por-tay*
important	important, -e	*en-por-tahn, -tahnt*
impossible	impossible	*en-po-seebl'*
in	dans	*dahn*

(*en* for feminine countries; *à* with def. art. for masculine countries; *à* for cities)

included	inclus, -e	*en-klŭ, -klŭz*
industry	industrie (f)	*en-dŭs-tree*
information	renseignement (m)	*rahn-sain-yuh-mahn*
inhabitant	habitant (m), -e (f)	*ah-bee-tahn, tahnt*
inn	auberge (f)	*oh-bairzh*
instead of	au lieu de	*oh lyuh duh*
inside	à l'intérieur	*ah-len-tair-yuhr*
intelligent	intelligent, -e	*en-tay-lee zhahn, -zhant*

(I am) interested!	Cela m'intéresse!	*suh-la men-tay-ress!*
interesting	intéressant, -e	*en-tay-reh-sahn, -sahnt*
interpreter	interprète (f)	*en-tair-prett*
into	dans	*dahn*
(to) introduce	présenter	*pray-zahn-tay*
invitation	invitation (f)	*en-vee-tass-yohn*
Ireland	Irlande (f)	*eer-lahnd*
Irish	irlandais, -e	*eer-lahn-day, -dayz*
is	est	*ay*
island	île (f)	*eel*
Israel	Israël	*eess-ra-el*
Israeli	israélien, -ienne	*eess-ra-ail-yen, -yenn*
it	il, elle	*eel, el*
its	son, sa, ses	*sohn, sa, say*
Italian	italien, -ne	*ee-tal-yen, -yenn*
Italy	Italie	*ee-ta-lee*

J

jacket	veste (f)	*vest*
jail	prison (f)	*pree-zohn*
January	janvier (m)	*zhan-v'yay*
Japan	Japon (m)	*zha-pohn*
Japanese	japonais, -e	*zha-po-nay, -ayz*
jewelry	bijouterie (f)	*bee-zhoot-ree*

Jew, Jewish	juif, juive	*zhweef, zhweev*
job	travail (m)	*tra-vye*
joke	plaisanterie (f)	*play-zahn-tree*
July	juillet (m)	*zhwee-yay*
June	juin (m)	*zhwen*
just	exactement	*ek-zak-tuh-mahn*

K

(to) keep	garder	*gar-day*
Keep out!	Défense d'entrer!	*day-fahns dahn-tray!*
Keep quiet!	Silence!	*see-lahnss!*
key	clé (f)	*klay*
kind	sorte (f)	*sort*
king	roi (m)	*rwah*
(to) kiss	embrasser	*ahn-bra-say*
kitchen	cuisine (f)	*kwee-zeen*
knee	genou (m)	*zhuh-noo*
knife	couteau (m)	*koo-toh*
know		
(to) have knowledge	savoir	*sa-vwahr*
(to) be acquainted with	connaître	*ko-naytr'*
Do you know (something)?	Savez-vous . . . ?	*sa-vay-voo . . . .?*

| **Do you know (someone)?** | Connaissez-vous . . . ? | *ko-nay-say-voo . . . ?* |
| **Who knows?** | Qui sait? | *kee say?* |

L

ladies' room	toilettes (f. pl.)	*twa-let*
lady	dame (f)	*dahm*
lake	lac (m)	*lahk*
lamb	agneau (m)	*ahn-yo*
land	terre (f)	*tair*
language	langue (f)	*lahng*
large	grand, -e	*grahn, grahnd*
last	dernier, ère	*dairn-yay, -yair*
late	tard	*tar*
later	plus tard	*plů tar*
lawyer	avocat (m. or f.)	*ah-vo-ka*
(to) learn	apprendre	*ah-prahndr'*
leather	cuir (m)	*kweer*
(to) leave	partir	*par-teer*
left	gauche	*gohsh*
leg	jambe (f)	*zhahnb*
lemon	citron (m)	*see-trohn*
(to) lend	prêter	*pray-tay*
less	moins	*mwen*
lesson	leçon (f)	*luh-sohn*

let's: Use the present tense verb form ending in *-ons* (the form that goes with the pronoun *nous*) by itself to express the idea of "Let's (do something)."

Let's go!	Partons!	*par-tohn!*
Let's wait a little.	Attendons un peu.	*ah-tahn-dohn zun puh.*
letter	lettre (f)	*letr'*
lettuce	laitue (f)	*lay-tů*
liberty	liberté (f)	*lee-bair-tay*
lieutenant	lieutenant (m)	*l'yuht-nahn*
life	vie (f)	*vee*
light	lumière (f)	*lům e-yair*
like	comme	*kom*
Like this.	Comme ça.	*kom-sa.*
(to) like	aimer	*ay-may*
linen	linge (m)	*lanzh*
lion	lion (m)	*l'yohn*
lip	lèvre (f)	*laivr'*
list	liste (f)	*leest*
(to) listen	écouter	*ay-koo-tay*
Listen!	Écoutez!	*ay-koo-tay!*
little (small)	petit, -e	*puh-tee, -teet*
a little	un peu	*un puh*
(to) live	vivre	*veevr'*
living room	salon (m)	*sa-lohn*
lobster	homard (m)	*o-mar*
long	long, longue	*lohn, lohng*
(to) look	regarder	*ruh-gar-day*
Look!	Regardez!	*ruh-gar-day!*
Look out!	Attention!	*ah-tahnss-yohn!*

(to) lose	perdre	*pairdr'*
lost	perdu	*pair-dŭ*
(a) lot	beaucoup	*bo-koo*
(to) love	aimer	*ay-may*
low	bas, -se	*ba, bahss*
luck	chance	*shah#ss*
Good luck!	Bonne chance!	*bunn shah#ss!*
luggage	bagage (m)	*ba-gahzh*
lunch	déjeuner (m)	*day-zhuh-nay*

M

machine	machine (f)	*ma-sheen*
madam	madame (f)	*ma-dahm*
made	fait, -e	*fay, fett*
maid	bonne (f)	*bunn*
mailbox	boîte aux lettres (f)	*bwaht oh letr'*
(to) make	faire	*fair*
man	homme (m)	*ohm*
manager	directeur (m)	*dee-rek-terr*
many	beaucoup	*bo-koo*
map	carte (f)	*kart*
March	mars (m)	*marss*
market	marché	*mar-shay*
married	marié, -e	*mar-yay*
mass	messe (f)	*mess*

matches	allumettes (f. pl)	*ah-lŭ-met*
matter	sujet (m)	*sŭ-zhay*
What's the matter?	Qu'est qu'il y a?	*kess keel ya?*
It does not matter.	Cela n'a pas d'impor- tance.	*suh-la na pa den-por-tahnss.*
May I?	Est-ce que je peux?	*ess kuh zhuh puh?*
May	mai (m)	*may*
maybe	peut-être	*puh-tetr'*
me	me, moi	*muh, mwah*
(to) mean	vouloir dire	*voo-lwahr deer*
meat	viande (f)	*vee-ahnd*
mechanic	mécanicien (m)	*may-ka-neess-yen*
medicine	médica- ment (m)	*may-dee-ka-mahn*
Mediterranean	Méditer- ranée (f)	*may-dee-tay-ra-nay*
(to) meet	rencontrer	*rahn-kohn-tray*
meeting	réunion (f)	*ray-ŭn-yohn*
member	membre (m)	*mahnbr'*
(to) mend	réparer	*ray-pa-ray*
men's room	toilettes (f. pl)	*twa-let*
menu	carte (f)	*kart*
message	message (m)	*may-sahzh*
meter	compteur (m)	*kohn-terr*
Mexico	Méxique (m)	*mek-seek*

middle	milieu (m)	*meel-yuh*
mile	mille (m)	*meel*
milk	lait (m)	*lay*
million	million (m)	*meel-yoh#*

mine	le mien,
	  la mienne
	les miens,
	  les miennes
		luh m'ye#,
		  la m'yen
		lay m'ye#,
		  lay m'yen

minister	pasteur (m)	*pahss-terr*
minute	minute (f)	*mee-nŭt*
Miss	Mademoi- selle (f)	*mahd-mwa-zell*
(to) miss	manquer	*mah#-kay*
mistake	erreur (f)	*ay-rerr*
Mr.	Monsieur	*muss-yuh*

**misunder-
  standing**
	malen-
	  tendu (m)
		ma-lah#-tah#-dŭ

Mrs.	Madame (f)	*ma-dahm*
model	modèle (m)	*mo-dell*
modern	moderne	*mo-dairn*
moment	moment (m)	*mo-mah#*
Monday	lundi (m)	*lu#-dee*
money	argent (m)	*ahr-zhah#*
monkey	singe (m)	*se#zh*
month	mois (m)	*mwah*
monument	monument (m)	*mo-nŭ-mah#*
moon	lune (f)	*lŭne*
more	plus	*plŭ*

morning	matin (m)	*ma-ten*
mosquito	moustique (m)	*moos-teek*
most	le plus	*luh plü*
mother	mère (f)	*mair*
mother-in-law	belle-mère (f)	*bell-mair*
motor	moteur (m)	*mo-terr*
motorcycle	moto-cyclette (f)	*mo-toh-see-klett*
mountain	montagne (f)	*mohn-tine*
mouth	bouche (f)	*boosh*
mouse	souris (f)	*soo-ree*
movie	film (m)	*feelm*
much	beaucoup	*bo-koo*
museum	musée (m)	*mü-zay*
music	musique (f)	*mü-zeek*
musician	musicien (m), -cienne (f)	*mü-zees-yen, -yen*

must: Use *il faut* with the infinitive of the principal verb.

I (you, he, etc.) must go.	Il faut partir.	*eel fo par-teer.*
I (you, he, etc.) must eat.	Il faut manger.	*eel fo mahn-zhay.*
mustache	moustache (f)	*moos-tahsh*
mustard	moutarde (f)	*moo-tard*
my	mon, ma, mes	*mohn, ma, may*

N

napkin	serviette (f)	*sairv-yet*
name	nom (m)	*nohn*

narrow	étroit, -e	*ay-trwa, -trwaht*
navy	marine (f)	*ma-reen*
near	près	*pray*
necessary	nécessaire	*nay-say-sair*
neck	cou (m)	*koo*
necktie	cravate (f)	*kra-vaht*
(to) need	avoir besoin de	*ah-vwahr buh-zwen duh*
neighborhood	voisinage (m)	*vwa-zee-nahzh*
nephew	neveu (m)	*nuh-vuh*
nervous	nerveux, -euse	*nair-vuh, -vuhz*
neutral	neutre	*nuhtr'*
never	ne . . . jamais	*nuh . . . zha-may*
Never mind.	Ça n'a pas d'importance.	*sa na pa d'en-por-tahnss.*
new	nouveau, -velle	*noo-vo, noo-vell*
news	nouvelles (f. pl)	*noo-vell*
New Year	Nouvel An	*noo-vel ahn*
next	prochain, -e	*pro-shen, shen*
nice	gentil, -ille	*zhahn-tee*
night	nuit (f)	*nwee*
nightclub	cabaret (m)	*ka-ba-ray*
nightgown	chemise de nuit (f)	*shuh-meez duh nwee*
nine	neuf	*nuff*
nineteen	dix-neuf	*deez-nuff*

ninety	quatre-vingt-dix	*ka-truh-ven-deess*
no!	non!	*nohn!*
no (adj.)	pas de . . .	*pa duh . . .*
no money	pas d'argent	*pa dar-zhahn*
no time	pas de temps	*pa duh tahn*
nobody	(ne) . . . personne	*(nuh) . . . pair-sunn*
noise	bruit (m)	*brwee*
noon	midi	*mee-dee*
normal	normal, -e	*nor-mahl*
north	nord (m)	*nor*
nose	nez (m)	*nay*
not	ne . . . pas	*nuh . . . pa*
I can not	je ne peux pas	*zhuh nuh puh pa*
Not yet.	Pas encore.	*pa zahn-kor.*
nothing	rien	*r'yan*
(to) notice	remarquer	*ruh-mar-kay*
noun	nom (m)	*nohn*
November	novembre (m)	*no-vahnbr'*
now	maintenant	*men-tuh-nahn*
nowhere	nulle part	*nůl par*
number	nombre (m)	*nohnbr'*
nurse	infirmière (f)	*en-feerm-yair*
nuts	noix	*nwa*

O

occasionally	à l'occasion	*ah lo-kaz-yohn*
occupied	occupé	*oh-kŭ-pay*
ocean	océan (m)	*oh-say-ahn*
o'clock	heure, -s (f)	*err*

(See page 25 for use.)

October	octobre (m)	*ok-tobr'*
of	de	*duh*
(to) offer	offrir	*o-freer*
office	bureau (m)	*bŭ-ro*
officer	officier (m)	*o-fees-yay*
often	souvent	*soo-vahn*
oil	huile (f)	*weel*
okay	d'accord	*da-kor*
old	vieux, vieille	*v'yuh, v'yay*
olive	olive (f)	*o-leev*
omelet	omelette (f)	*om-let*
on	sur	*sŭr*
once	une fois	*ŭne fwa*
At once!	Tout de suite!	*toot sweet!*
one	un, une	*un, ŭne*
one way (traffic)	sens unique	*sahn zŭ-neek*
on time	à l'heure	*ah lerr*
onion	oignon	*on-yohn*
only	seulement	*suhl-mahn*
open	ouvert, -e	*oo'vair, -vairt*

(to) open	ouvrir	*oo-vreer*
open air	plein air (m)	*plen nair*
opera	opéra (m)	*oh-pay-ra*
opinion	opinion (f)	*oh-peen-yohn*
in my opinion	à mon avis	*ah mohn na-vee*
opportunity	occasion (f)	*oh-kaz-yohn*
opposite	en face	*ahn fahss*
or	ou	*oo*
orange	orange	*o-rahnzh*
orchestra	orchestre (m)	*or-kestr'*
order	ordre (m)	*ordr'*
(to) order	commander	*ko-mahn-day*
in order to	afin de	*ah-fen duh*
original	original, -e	*oh-ree-zhee-nahl*
other	autre	*ohtr'*
ought	devoir	*duh-vwahr*
you ought to . . .	Vous devriez . . .	*voo duh-vree-yay . . .*

See "should" for complete list of forms.

our	notre	*notr'*
outside	à l'extérieur	*ah lex-tair-yerr*
over (above)	au-dessus	*ohd-sü*
over (finished)	fini, -e	*fee-nee*
overcoat	manteau (m)	*mahn-toh*
over there	là-bas	*la-ba*
overweight	trop lourd, -e	*tro loor, loord*
(to) owe	devoir	*duh-vwahr*

own	propre	*prohpr*
owner	propriétaire (m)	*pro-pree-yay-tair*
ox, oxen	boeuf, boeufs	*buhf, buh*
oyster	huître (f)	*weetr'*

P

package	paquet (m)	*pa-kay*
paid	payé, -e	*pay-yay*
pain	douleur (f)	*doo-lurr*
(to) paint	peindre	*pen-dr'*
painting	peinture (f)	*pen-tůr*
palace	palais (m)	*pa-lay*
pan	casserole (f)	*kass-roll*
paper	papier (m)	*pap-yay*
parade	défilé (m)	*day-fee-lay*
Pardon me!	Excusez-moi!	*ex-ků-zay-mwa!*
Parisian	Parisien, -ne	*pa-rees-yen, -yenn*
(to) park	parquer	*par-kay*
park	parc (m)	*park*
parents	parents (m. pl)	*pa-rahn*
part	partie (f)	*par-tee*
participle	participe (m)	*par-tee-seep*
partner	associé (m)	*ah-sohss-yay*
party (entertainment)	partie (f)	*par-tee*
party (political)	parti (m)	*par-tee*

passenger (train, bus)	voyageur (m), -euse (f)	*vwa-ya-zherr, -zhehz*
passenger (boat, plane)	passager (m), -ère (f)	*pa-sa-zhay, -zhair*
passport	passeport (m)	*pass-por*
past	passé, -e	*pa-say*
(to) pay	payer	*pay-yay*
peace	paix	*pay*
pen	stylo (m)	*stee-lo*
pencil	crayon (m)	*kray-yohn*
people	des gens (f. pl)	*day zhahn*
percent	pourcentage (m)	*poor-sahn-tazh*
perfect	parfait, -e	*par-fay, -fait*
perfume	parfum (m)	*par-fen*
perhaps	peut-être	*puh-tetr'*
permanent	permanent, -e	*pair-ma-nahn, -nahnt*
permitted	permis, -e	*pair-mee, -meez*
person	personne (f)	*pair-sunn*
phone	téléphone (m)	*tay-lay-fohn*
photo	photo (f)	*fo-toh*
piano	piano (m)	*pee-ah-no*
(to) pick up	ramasser	*ra-ma-say*
picture	tableau (m)	*ta-blo*
piece	morceau (m)	*mor-so*
pier	quai (m)	*kay*
pill	pilule (f)	*pee-lŭl*
pillow	oreiller	*o-ray-yay*

pin	épingle (f)	*ay-pengl'*
pink	rose	*rohz*
pipe (smoking)	pipe (f)	*peep*
place	endroit (m)	*ahn-drwa*
plain	simple	*senpl'*
plans	projets (m. pl)	*pro-zhay*
plane	avion (m)	*ahv-yohn*
planet	planète (f)	*pla-net*
plant (botanical)	plante (f)	*plahnt*
plant (factory)	usine (f)	*ů-zeen*
plate	assiette (f)	*ahss-yet*
play (theater)	pièce (f)	*p'yess*
(to) play	jouer	*zhoo-ay*
plastic	plastique (f)	*plahss-teek*
pleasant	agréable	*ah-gray-abl'*
please	s'il vous plaît	*seel voo play*
pleasure	plaisir (m)	*play-zeer*
plural	pluriel (m)	*plůr-yell*
pocket	poche (f)	*pohsh*
poetry	poésie (f)	*po-ay-zee*
(to) point	indiquer	*en-dee-kay*
police	police (f)	*po-leess*
policeman	agent de police (m)	*ah-zhahn duh po-leess*
poisonous	vénéneux, -neuse	*vay-nay-nuh, -nuhz*
police station	commissariat de police (m)	*ko-mee-sahr-ya duh po-leess*

polite	poli, -e	*po-lee*
poor	pauvre	*pohvr'*
pope	pape (m)	*pahp*
popular	populaire	*po-pŭ-lair*
pork	porc (m)	*por*
Portugal	Portugal (m)	*por-tŭ-gahl*
possible	possible	*po-seebl'*
post card	carte postale (f)	*kart pohs-tahl*
post office	bureau de poste (m)	*bŭ-ro duh post*
potato	pomme de terre (f)	*pom duh tair*
pound (weight)	livre (f)	*leevr'*
(to) practice	pratiquer	*pra-tee-kay*
(to) prefer	préférer	*pray-fay-ray*
pregnant	enceinte	*ahn-sent*
present (time)	présent (m)	*pray-zahn*
present (gift)	cadeau (m)	*ka-doh*
president	président (m)	*pray-zee-dahn*
(to) press	repasser	*ruh-pa-say*
pretty	joli, -e	*zho-lee*
(to) prevent	empêcher	*ahn-pay-shay*
previously	antérieurement	*ahn-tair-yurr-mahn*
price	prix (m)	*pree*
priest	prêtre (m)	*pretr'*
prince	prince (m)	*prenss*
princess	princesse (f)	*pren-sess*

principal	principal, -e	*pren-see-pahl*
prison	prison (f)	*pree-zohn*
private	privé, -e	*pree-vay*
probably	probablement	*pro-ba-bluh-mahn*
problem	problème (m)	*pro-blaym*
production	production (f)	*pro-důks-yohn*
profession	profession (f)	*pro-fess-yohn*
professor	professeur (m)	*pro-fay-serr*
program	programme (m)	*pro-grahm*
(to) promise	promettre	*pro-mettr'*
promised	promis, -e	*pro-mee, -meez*
pronoun	pronom (m)	*pro-nohn*
propaganda	propagande (f)	*pro-pa-gahnd*
property	propriété (f)	*pro-pree-ay-tay*
Protestant	Protestant, -e	*pro-tess-tahn, -tahnt*
public	public, -que	*pů-bleek*
publicity	publicité (f)	*pů-blee-see-tay*
publisher	éditeur (m)	*ay-dee-terr*
(to) pull	tirer	*tee-ray*
pure	pur, -e	*půr*
(to) purchase	acheter	*ash-tay*
purple	violet, -te	*vee-oh-lay, -let*
purse	sac (m)	*sak*
(to) push	pousser	*poo-say*
(to) put	mettre	*mettr'*
(to) put on	mettre	*mettr'*

Q

quality	qualité (f)	*ka-lee-tay*
queen	reine (f)	*ren*
question	question (f)	*kess-t'yohn*
quick	rapide	*ra-peed*
quickly	vite	*veet*
quiet	calme	*kahlm*
quite	tout à fait	*too ta fay*

R

rabbi	rabin (m)	*ra-ben*
rabbit	lapin (m)	*la-pen*
race (contest)	course (f)	*koorss*
radio	radio (f)	*rad-yo*
railroad	chemin de fer (m)	*shuh-men duh fair*
rain	pluie (f)	*plwee*
It's raining.	Il pleut.	*eel pluh.*
raincoat	imperméable (m)	*en-pair-may-ahbl'*
rapidly	rapidement	*ra-peed-mahn*
rarely	rarement	*rahr-mahn*
rate	taux (m)	*toh*
rather	de préférence	*duh pray-fay-rahnss*
I would rather.	J'aimerais mieux.	*zhaim-ray m'yuh.*

razor	rasoir (m)	*ra-zwahr*
(to) read	lire	*leer*
ready	prêt, -e	*pray, prett*
really	vraiment	*vray-mahn*
reason	raison (f)	*ray-zohn*
receipt	reçu (m)	*ruh-sü*
(to) receive	recevoir	*ruh-suh-vwahr*
recently	récemment	*ray-sa-mahn*
récipe	recette (f)	*ruh-set*
(to) recognize	reconnaître	*ruh-ko-naitr'*
(to) recommend	recommander	*ruh-ko-mahn-day*
red	rouge	*roozh*
refrigerator	réfrigérateur (m)	*ray-free-zhay-ra-turr*
(to) refuse	refuser	*ruh-fü-zay*
(My) regards to . . .	Mes respects à . . .	*may reh-spay ah . . .*
regular	régulier, -ère	*ray-gül-yay, -yair*
religion	religion (f)	*ruh-leezh-yohn*
(to) remain	rester	*ress-tay*
(to) remember	se rappeler	*suh rap-lay*
(to) rent	louer	*lway*
(to) repair	réparer	*ray-pa-ray*
(to) repeat	répéter	*ray-pay-tay*
Repeat, please!	Répétez, s'il vous plaît!	*ray-pay-tay, seel voo play!*
report	rapport (m)	*ra-por*
(to) represent	représenter	*ruh-pray-zahn-tay*

representative	représentant, -e	*ruh-pray-zahn-tahn, -tahnt*
responsible	responsable	*res-pohn-sahbl'*
resident	résident, -e	*ray-zee-dahn, -dahnt*
(to) rest	se reposer	*suh ruh-po-say*
restaurant	restaurant (m)	*res-toh-rahn*
(to) return	revenir	*ruh-vuh-neer*
revolution	révolution (f)	*ray-vo-lŭss-yohn*
reward	récompense (f)	*ray-kohn-pahns*
rice	riz (m)	*ree*
rich	riche	*reesh*
(to) ride)	monter à	*mohn-tay ah*
right (direction)	droit, droite	*drwah, drwaht*
To the right!	A droite!	*ah drwaht!*
right (correct)	exact, -e	*ex-zakt*
You are right!	Vous avez raison!	*voo za-vay ray-zohn!*
Right away!	Tout de suite!	*tood-sweet!*
That's right!	C'est vrai!	*say vray!*
ring	bague (f)	*bahg*
riot	émeute (f)	*eh-mert*
river	fleuve (m)	*fluhv*
road	route (f)	*root*
roof	toit (m)	*twa*
room	chambre (f)	*shahnbr'*
room service	service de restaurant (m)	*sair-veess duh res-toh-rahn*

round trip	aller retour (m)	*ah-lay ruh-toor*
route	trajet (m)	*tra-zhay*
rug	tapis (m)	*ta-pee*
(to) run	courir	*koo-reer*
Russia	Russie (f)	*rŭ-see*
Russian	Russe	*rŭss*

S

sad	triste	*treest*
safe	sûr, -e	*sŭr*
safety pin	épingle anglaise (f)	*ay-pengl' ahn-glayz*
sailor	marin (m)	*ma-ren*
saint	saint, -e	*sen, sentt*
salad	salade (f)	*sa-lahd*
salary	salaire (m)	*sa-lair*
sale	solde	*sold*
same	même	*mem*
Saturday	samedi	*sam-dee*
(to) say	dire	*deer*
scenery	paysage (m)	*pay-ee-zahzh*
school	école (f)	*ay-kol*
scissors	ciseaux (m. pl)	*see-zo*
Scotch	écossais, -e	*ay-ko-say, -sayz*
Scotland	Écosse (f)	*ay-koss*
sea	mer (f)	*mair*

seafood	fruits de mer (m. pl)	*frwee duh mair*
season	saison (f)	*say-zohn*
seat	place (f)	*plahss*
secretary	secrétaire (f)	*suh-kray-tair*
(to) see	voir	*vwahr*
(to) seem	sembler	*sahn-blay*
It would seem . . .	On dirait . . .	*ohn dee-ray . .*
seen	vu	*vǔ*
seldom	rarement	*rahr-mahn*
(to) sell	vendre	*vahndr'*
(to) send	envoyer	*ahn-vwa-yay*
(to) send for	envoyer chercher	*ahn-vwa-yay shair-shay*
September	septembre (m)	*sep-tahnbr'*
serious	sérieux, -se	*sair-yuh, -yuhz*
service	service (m)	*sair-veess*
seven	sept	*set*
seventeen	dix-sept	*deess-set*
seventy	soixante-dix	*swa-sahnt-deess*
several	plusieurs	*plǔz-yurr*
shampoo	shampooing (m)	*shahn-pwen*
shark	requin (m)	*ruh-ken*
she	elle	*el*
ship	bateau (m)	*ba-toh*
shirt	chemise (f)	*shuh-meez*
shoe	chaussure (f)	*sho-sǔr*

| shop | magasin (m) | *ma-ga-zen* |
| short | court, -e | *koor, koort* |

should: Use the appropriate one of the following forms of *devoir* with the infinitive of the principal verb.

I should . . .	je devrais . . .	*zhuh duh-vray . . .*
you should . . .	voux de- vriez . . .	*voo duh-vree-ay . . .*
he should . . .	il devrait . . .	*eel duh-vray . . .*
she should . . .	elle de- vrait . . .	*el duh-vray . . .*
we should . . .	nous de- vrions . . .	*noo duh-vree- yohn . . .*
they (m) should . . .	ils de- vràient . . .	*eel duh-vray . . .*
they (f) should . . .	elles de- vraient . . .	*el duh-vray . . .*
I should leave.	Je devrais partir.	*zhuh duh-vray par- teer.*
shoulder	épaule (f)	*ay-pohl*
show	spectacle (m)	*spek-tahkl'*
(to) show	montrer	*mohn-tray*
Show me!	Montrez-moi!	*mohn-tray-mwa!*
shower	douche (f)	*doosh*
shrimps	crevettes (f. pl)	*kruh-vet*
shut	fermé, -e	*fair-may*
(to) shut	fermer	*fair-may*
sick	malade	*ma-lahd*
(to) sign	signer	*seen-yay*

silk	soie (f)	*swa*
silver	argent (m)	*ar-zhahn*
since	depuis	*duh-pwee*
sincerely	sincèrement	*sen-sair-mahn*
(to) sing	chanter	*shahn-tay*
singer	chanteur (m), -euse (f)	*shahn-terr, -tuhz*
sir	monsieur (m)	*muss-yuh*
sister	soeur (f)	*surr*
sister-in-law	belle-soeur (f)	*bell-serr*
Sit down!	Asseyez-vous!	*ah-say-yay-voo!*
six	six	*seess*
sixteen	seize	*sayz*
sixty	soixante	*swa-sahnt*
size	taille (f)	*tye*
(to) skate	patiner	*pa-tee-nay*
(to) ski	skier	*skee-yay*
skin	peau (f)	*po*
skirt	jupe (f)	*zhůp*
sky	ciel (m)	*s'yell*
(to) sleep	dormir	*dor-meer*
sleeve	manche (f)	*mahnsh*
slowly	lentement	*lahnt-mahn*
small	petit, -e	*puh-tee, -teet*
(to) smoke	fumer	*fů-may*
snow	neige (f)	*nayzh*
so	donc	*dohnk*

soap	savon (m)	*sa-vohn*
socks	chaussettes (f. pl)	*sho-set*
sofa	canapé (m)	*ka-na-pay*
soft	doux, douce	*doo, dooss*
soldier	soldat (m)	*sol-da*
some (a little)	un peu de	*un puh duh*
somebody	quelqu'un	*kelk-un*
something	quelque chose	*kel-kuh shohz*
sometimes	quelquefois	*kel-kuh-fwah*
somewhere	quelque part	*kel-kuh par*
son	fils (m)	*feess*
son-in-law	beau-fils (m)	*bo-feess*
song	chanson (f)	*shahn-sohn*
soon	bientôt	*b'yen-toh*
(I am) sorry.	Je regrette.	*zhuh ruh-grett.*
soup	soupe (f)	*soop*
south	sud (m)	*sŭd*
South America	Amérique du Sud	*ah-may-reek dŭ sŭd*
souvenir	souvenir (m)	*soo-vuh-neer*
Spain	Espagne	*ess-pahn-yuh*
Spanish	espagnol, -e	*ess-pan-yohl*
(to) speak	parler	*par-lay*
special	spécial, -e	*spays-yahl*
(to) spend	dépenser	*day-pahn-say*
spoon	cuiller (f)	*kwee-yair*

sport	sport (m)	*spor*
spring	printemps (m)	*pren-tahn*
stairs	escalier (m)	*ess-kahl-yay*
stamp	timbre (m)	*tenbr'*
star	étoile (f)	*ay-twahl*
(to) start	commencer	*ko-mahn-say*
state	état (m)	*ay-ta*
station	gare (f)	*gar*
statue	statue (f)	*sta-tǔ*
(to) stay	rester	*res-tay*
steak	steak (m)	*stek*
steel	acier (m)	*ass-yay*
steward	steward (m)	*stoo-ward*
stewardess	hôtesse (f)	*o-tess*
still	encore	*ahn-kor*
stockings	bas (m. pl)	*ba*
stone	pierre (f)	*p'yair*
Stop!	Arrêtez!	*ah-ray-tay!*
Stop it!	Assez!	*ah-say!*
store	magasin (m)	*ma-ga-zen*
storm	orage (m)	*o-rahzh*
story	histoire (f)	*ess-twahr*
straight ahead	tout droit	*too drwa*
strange	étrange	*ay-trahnzh*
street	rue (f)	*rǔ*
string	corde (f)	*kord*
strong	fort, -e	*for, fort*

student	étudiant (m), -e (f)	*ay-tŭd-yahn, -yahnt*
(to) study	étudier	*ay-tŭd-yay*
style	style	*steel*
subway	métro (m)	*may-tro*
suddenly	tout d'un coup	*too dun koo*
suede	suède (m)	*swaid*
sugar	sucre (m)	*sŭkr'*
suit	complet (m)	*kohn-play*
suitcase	valise (f)	*va-leez*
summer	été (m)	*ay-tay*
sun	soleil (m)	*so-lay*
Sunday	dimanche (m)	*dee-mahnsh*
sure	sûr, -e	*sŭr*
surely	sûrement	*sŭr-mahn*
surprise	surprise (f)	*sŭr-preez*
sweater	sweater (m)	*sweater*
sweet	doux, douce	*doo, dooss*
(to) swim	nager	*na-zhay*
swimming pool	piscine (f)	*pee-seen*
swimsuit	maillot de bain (m)	*may-yo duh ben*
Swiss	suisse	*sweess*
Switzerland	Suisse (f)	*sweess*

T

| table | table (f) | *tahbl'* |
| tablecloth | nappe (f) | *napp* |

tailor	tailleur (m)	*ta-yurr*
(to) take	prendre	*prahndr'*
take away	enlever	*ahn-luh-vay*
(to) take care of	prendre soin de	*prahndr' swen duh*
take a walk (ride)	faire une promenade	*fair ŭne prom-nahd*
(to) talk	parler	*par-lay*
tall	grand, -e	*grahn, grahnd*
tank	réservoir (m)	*ray-zair-vwar*
tape	ruban (m)	*rŭ-bahn*
tape recorder	magnétophone (m)	*man-yay-toh-fohn*
tax	impôt (m)	*en-po*
taxi	taxi (m)	*tahk-see*
tea	thé (m)	*tay*
(to) teach	enseigner	*ahn-sayn-yay*
teacher	professeur (m)	*pro-fay-serr*
team	équipe (f)	*ay-keep*
telegram	télégramme (m)	*tay-lay-grahm*
telephone	téléphone (m)	*tay-lay-fohn*
television	télévision (f)	*tay-lay-veez-yohn*
(to) tell	dire	*deer*
Tell me . . .	Dites-moi . . .	*deet-mwa . . .*
Tell him (her) . . .	Dites-lui . . .	*deet-lwee . . .*
temple	temple (m)	*tahnpl'*
temperature	température (f)	*tahn-pay-ra-tŭr*

ten	dix	*deess*
tennis	tennis (m)	*tay-neess*
tense	temps (m)	*tahn*
past tense	temps passé	*tahn pa-say*
future tense	temps futur	*tahn fŭ-tŭr*
terrace	terrasse (f)	*tay-rass*
terrible	terrible	*tay-reebl'*
than	que	*kuh*
thank you	merci	*mair-see*
that	que	*kuh*
the	le, la, les	*luh, la, lay*
theatre	théâtre (m)	*tay-ahtr'*
their	leur, leurs	*lerr*
them (dir. obj.)	les	*lay*
(to) them	eux	*uh*
then	alors	*ah-lor*
there	là	*la*
There is . . . There are . . .	Il y a	*eel ee ya . . .*
these	ces, ceux-ci, celles-ci	*say, suh-see, sell-see*
they	ils (m), elles (f)	*eel, ell*
thin	mince	*menss*
thing	chose (f)	*shohz*
(to) think	penser	*pahn-say*
Do you think . . . ?	Pensez- vous . . . ?	*pahn-say-voo . . . ?*

I think . . .	Je pense . . .	zhuh pahnss . . .
third	troisième	trwahz-yem
(I am) thirsty.	J'ai soif.	zhay swahf.
thirteen	treize	trayz
thirty	trente	trahnt
this	ce, cette, celui-ci, celle-ci	suh, set, suh-lwee-see, sell-see
those	ces, ceux-là, celles-la	say, suh-la, sell-la
thousand	mille	meel
thread	fil (m)	feel
three	trois	trwa
throat	gorge (f)	gorzh
Thursday	jeudi	zhuh-dee
ticket	billet (m)	bee-yay
tie	cravate (f)	kra-vaht
tiger	tigre (m)	teegr'
time	temps (m)	tahn
tip	pourboire (m)	poor-bwar
tire	pneu (m)	pnuh
tired	fatigué, -e	fa-tee-gay
to (direction)	à	ah
to (in order to)	afin de	ah-fen duh
toast	toast (m)	tohst
tobacco	tabac (m)	ta-ba
today	aujourd'hui	oh-zhoor-dwee

toe	doigt de pied (m)	*dwa duh p'yay*
together	ensemble	*ahn-sahnbl'*
tomato	tomate (f)	*to-maht*
tomorrow	demain	*duh-men*
tomb	tombe (f)	*tohnb*
tongue	langue (f)	*lahng*
tonight	ce soir (m)	*suh swahr*
too (also)	aussi	*o-see*
too (excessive)	trop	*tro*
tool	outil (m)	*oo-tee*
tooth	dent (f)	*dahn*
toothbrush	brosse à dents	*brohss ah dahn*
toothpaste	dentifrice (m)	*dahn-tee-freess*
touring	en visitant	*ahn vee-zee-tan*
tourist	touriste	*too-reest*
toward	vers	*vair*
towel	serviette (f)	*sairv-yet*
tower	tour (f)	*toor*
town	ville (f)	*veel*
toy	jouet (m)	*zhoo-ay*
traffic	circulation (f)	*seer-kŭ-lass-yohn*
train	train (m)	*tran*
translation	traduction (f)	*tra-dŭks-yohn*
(to) travel	voyager	*vwa-ya-zhay*
travel agent	agent de voyage (m)	*ah-zhahn duh vwa-yahzh*
traveler	voyageur (m)	*vwa-ya-zherr*

treasurer	trésorier (m)	*tray-zohr-yay*
tree	arbre (m)	*ahrbr'*
trip	voyage (m)	*vwa-yahzh*
trouble	difficulté (f)	*dee-fee-kŭl-tay*
trousers	pantalon (m)	*pahn-ta-lohn*
truck	camion (m)	*kam-yohn*
true	vrai, -e	*vray*
truth	vérité (f)	*vay-ree-tay*
(to) try, try on	essayer	*ay-say-yay*
Tuesday	mardi	*mar-dee*
Turkey	Turquie	*tŭr-kee*
Turkish	turque	*tŭrk*
(to) turn	tourner	*toor-nay*
(to) turn off	éteindre	*ay-tendr'*
(to) turn on	allumer	*ah-lŭ-may*
twelve	douze	*dooz*
two	deux	*duh*
typewriter	machine à écrire (f)	*ma-sheen ah ay-kreer*
typical	typique	*tee-peek*

U

ugly	laid, -e	*lay, laid*
umbrella	parapluie (m)	*pa-ra-plwee*
uncle	oncle (m)	*ohnkl'*
under	sous	*soo*
underneath	en dessous	*ahn duh-soo*

(to) understand	comprendre	*kohn-prahndr'*
Do you understand?	Comprenez-vous?	*kohn-pruh-nay-voo?*
I don't understand.	Je ne comprends pas.	*zhuh nuh kohn-prahn pa.*
underwear	sous-vêtement (m)	*soo-vet-mahn*
unfortunately	malheureusement	*ma-luh-ruhz-mahn*
uniform	uniforme (m)	*ŭ-nee-form*
United States	Etats-Unis (m. pl)	*ay-ta-zŭ-nee*
in the United States	aux Etats-Unis	*oh zay-ta-zŭ-nee*
United Nations	Nations Unies (f. pl)	*nass-yohn-zŭ-nee*
university	université (f)	*ŭ-nee-vair-see-tay*
until	jusqu'à	*zhŭs-ka*
up (upstairs)	en haut	*ahn oh*
Get up!	Levez-vous!	*luh-vay-voo!*
urgent	urgent, -e	*ŭr-zhahn, -zhahnt*
us	nous	*noo*
(to) use	employer	*ahn-plwa-yay*
useful	utile	*ŭ-teel*
usually	d'habitude	*da-bee-tŭd*

V

vacant	libre	*leebr'*
(on) vacation	en vacances	*ahn-va-kahns*

vaccination	vaccination (f)	*vak-see-nass-yohn*
valley	vallée (f)	*va-lay*
valuable	de valeur	*duh va-luhr*
value	valeur (f)	*va-luhr*
vanilla	vanille (f)	*va-nee*
various	divers, -e	*dee-vair, -vairss*
vegetable	légume (m)	*lay-gůme*
verb	verbe (m)	*vairb*
very	très	*tray*
very well	très bien	*tray b'yen*
view	vue (f)	*vů*
village	village (m)	*vee-lahzh*
vinegar	vinaigre (m)	*vee-naigr'*
visa	visa (m)	*vee-za*
visit	visite (f)	*vee-zeet*
visitor	visiteur (m), -euse (f)	*vee-zee-terr, -terz*
(to) visit (a place)	visiter	*vee-zee-tay*
(to) visit (a person)	rendre visite à	*rahndr' vee-zeet ah*
violin	violon (m)	*vee-oh-lohn*
voice	voix (f)	*vwa*
volcano	volcan (m)	*vol-kahn*
voyage	voyage (m)	*vwa-yahzh*

W

waist	taille (f)	*tye*
(to) wait	attendre	*ah-tahndr'*

Wait here!	Attendez ici!	*ah-tahn-day zee-see!*
Waiter!	Garçon!	*gar-sohn!*
Waitress!	Mademoiselle!	*mahd-mwa-zell!*
a waitress	une serveuse (f)	*ůne sair-vuhz*
(to) walk	marcher	*mar-shay*
wall	mur	*můr*
wallet	portefeuille (m)	*port-foy*
(to) want	vouloir	*voo-lwahr*
I want	je veux	*zhuh vuh*
you want	vous voulez	*voo voo-lay*
he wants	il veut	*eel vuh*
she wants	elle veut	*el vuh*
we want	nous voulons	*noo voo-lohn*
they (m) want	ils veulent	*eel vuhl*
they (f) want	elles veulent	*el vuhl*
Do you want . . . ?	Voulez-vous . . . ?	*voo-lay-voo . . . ?*
war	guerre (f)	*gair*
warm	chaud, -e	*shoh, shohd*
(I) was	j'étais	*zhay-tay*
he was	il était	*eel ay-tay*
it was	c'était	*say-tay*
she was	elle était	*el ay-tay*
(to) wash	laver	*la-vay*
watch	montre (f)	*mohntr'*
Watch out!	Faites attention!	*fet ah-tahnss-yohn*

water	eau (f)	*oh*
water color	aquarelle (f)	*ah-kwa-rell*
way	chemin (m)	*shuh-men*
in this way	de cette manière (f)	*duh set mahn-yair*
we	nous	*noo*
weak	faible	*faibl'*
(to) wear	porter	*por-tay*
weather	temps (m)	*tahn*
wedding	mariage (m)	*ma-ree-ahzh*
week	semaine (f)	*suh-men*
weekend	week-end	*week-end*
(to) weigh	peser	*puh-zay*
weight	poids (m)	*pwa*
Welcome!	Bienvenue!	*b'yen-vuh-nŭ!*
(you are) welcome	il n'y a pas de quoi	*eel nee ya pa duh kwa*
well	bien	*b'yen*
went		
I went	je suis allé	*zhuh swee za-lay*
you went	vous êtes allé	*voo zett ah-lay*
he went	il est allé	*eel ay ta-lay*
she went	elle est allée	*el ay ta-lay*
we went	nous sommes allés	*noo som za-lay*
they (m) went	ils sont allés	*eel sohn ta-lay*
they (f) went	elles sont allées	*el sohn ta-lay*

were

we were	nous étions	*noo zait-yohn*
you were	vous étiez	*voo zait-yay*
they (m) were	ils étaient	*eel zay-tay*
they (f) were	elles étaient	*el zay-tay*
west	ouest (m)	*west*
what	que	*kuh*
What?	Quoi?	*kwa?*
What's the matter?	Qu'est-ce qu'il y a?	*kess keel ee ya?*
What time is it?	Quelle heure est-il?	*kel err ay-teel?*
What do you want?	Que voulez-vous?	*kuh voo-lay-voo?*
wheel	roue (f)	*roo*
when	quand	*kahn*
where	où	*oo*
wherever	partout où	*par-too oo*
Where to?	Quelle direction?	*kel dee-reks-yohn?*
whether	si	*see*
which (sub.)	qui	*kee*
which (obj.)	que	*kuh*
while	alors que	*ah-lor kuh*
for a while	pendant un moment	*pahn-dahn tun mo-mahn*
white	blanc, blanche	*blahn, blahnsh*
who	qui	*kee*
whole	entier, -ière	*ahnt-yay, -yair*
whom	que	*kuh*

why	pourquoi	*poor-kwa*
Why not?	Pourquoi pas?	*poor-kwa pa?*
wide	large	*larzh*
widow	veuve (f)	*vuhv*
widower	veuf (m)	*vuhf*
wife	femme (f)	*fahm*
wild	sauvage	*so-vahzh*

will: The future is formed by adding the appropriate ending to the final *r* of the infinitive: *(je) -ai, (il, elle) -a, (nous) -ons, (vous) -ez, (ils, elles) -ont.* (Or you can express the future idea by using a form of *aller,* "to go," with the infinitive. See p. 148.) Several important common verbs have special forms for the future, but they all have the regular ending: *(être) je serai; (avoir) j'aurai; (aller) j'irai; (venir) je viendrai; (faire) je ferai.*

I will speak	je parlerai	*zhuh par-luh-ray*
Will you finish?	Finirez-vous?	*fee-nee-ray-voo?*
He won't allow it.	Il ne le per-mettra pas.	*eel nuh luh pair-met-ra pa.*
to win	gagner	*gahn-yay*
wind	vent (m)	*vahn*
window	fenêtre (f)	*fuh-netr'*
wine	vin (m)	*van*
winter	hiver (m)	*ee-vair*
(to) wish	désirer	*day-zee-ray*
without	sans	*sahn*
wolf	loup (m)	*loo*
woman	femme (f)	*fahm*

wonderful	merveilleux, -se	*mair-vay-yuh, -yuhz*
won't (See will.)		
wood, woods	bois (m)	*bwa*
wool	laine (f)	*lain*
word	mot (m)	*mo*
work	travail (m)	*tra-vye*
(to) work	travailler	*tra-va-yay*
world	monde (m)	*mohnd*
(Don't) worry!	Ne vous en faites pas!	*nuh voo zahn fait pa!*
worse	pire	*peer*

would: Express the idea of "would" by adding the appropriate one of the following endings to the final *r* of the infinitive: *(je) -ais, (il, elle) -ait, (nous) -ions, (vous) -iez, (ils, elles) aient.*

you would write	vous écririez	*voo zay-kreer-yay*
I would like . . .	je voudrais . . .	*zhuh voo-dray . . .*
would you like . . . ?	Voudriez-vous . . . ?	*voo-dree-ay voo . . . ?*
wrist	poignet (m)	*pwahn-yay*
(to) write	écrire	*ay-kreer*
Write it.	Écrivez-le.	*ay-kree-vay luh.*
writer	écrivain	*ay-kree-ven*

| wrong | faux, fausse | *fo, fohss* |
| **I am wrong.** | J'ai tort. | *zhay tor.* |

Y

year	année	*ah-nay*
yellow	jaune	*zhohn*
yes	oui	*wee*
yesterday	hier	*ee-yair*
yet	pourtant	*poor-tahπ*
not yet	pas encore	*pa zahπ-kor*
you	vous	*voo*
young	jeune	*zhuhn*
your	votre	*votr'*
yours	le vôtre	*luh vohtr'*

Z

zipper	fermeture éclair (f)	*fairm-tŭr ay-klair*
zoo	zoo (m)	*zo*
zone	zone (f)	*zohn*

POINT TO THE ANSWER

For speedy reference and, when in doubt, to get a clear answer to a question you have just asked, show the following sentence to the person you are addressing and let him or her point to the answer to your question. The sentence in

French after the arrow asks the other person to point to the answer.

 Veuillez indiquer ci-dessous la réponse à ma question. Merci.

Oui.
Yes.

Non.
No.

Peut-être.
Perhaps.

Certainement.
Certainly.

C'est bien.
All right.

Je comprends.
I understand.

Je ne comprends pas.
I don't understand.

Qu'est-ce que vous désirez?
What do you want?

Je sais.
I know.

Je ne sais pas.
I don't know.

Encore.
Again (*or*) more.

Assez.
Enough.

Ouvert.
Open.

Fermé.
Closed.

Trop.
Too much.

Pas assez.
Not enough.

Maintenant.
Now.

Plus tard.
Later.

Trop tôt.
Too early.

Trop tard.
Too late.

Aujourd'hui.
Today.

Demain.
Tomorrow.

Hier.
Yesterday.

Ce soir.
Tonight.

Hier soir.
Last night.

Demain soir.
Tomorrow night.

Cette semaine.
This week.

La semaine passée.
Last week.

La semaine prochaine.
Next week.

C'est possible.
It's possible.

Ce n'est pas possible.
It's not possible.

C'est entendu.
It is agreed.

C'est défendu.
It is forbidden.

Ce n'est pas bien.
It isn't good.

Très bien.
Very good.

C'est près.
It's near.

Très loin.
Very far.

Trop loin.
Too far.

C'est tout.
That's all.

Ici.
Here.

Là-bas.
Over there.

Défense d'entrer.
No admittance.

Tournez à gauche.
Turn left.

Tournez à droite.
Turn right.

Allez tout droit.
Go straight ahead.

Venez avec moi.
Come with me.

Suivez-moi.
Follow me.

Allons.
Let's go.

Nous sommes arrivés.
We have arrived.

Arrêtez ici.
Stop here.

Attendez-moi.
Wait for me.

Je ne peux pas.
I cannot.

J'attendrai.
I will wait.

Je dois partir.
I must go.

Revenez plus tard.
Come back later.

Je reviendrai tout de suite.
I'll be right back.

Il n'est pas ici.
He is not here.

Elle n'est pas ici.
She is not here.

Mon nom est _____ .
My name is _____ .

Votre nom?
Your name?

Numéro de téléphone?
Telephone number?

Adresse?
Address?

lundi
Monday

mardi
Tuesday

mercredi
Wednesday

jeudi
Thursday

vendredi
Friday

samedi
Saturday

dimanche
Sunday

A _____ heures.
At _____ o'clock.

**C'est _____ francs
_____ centimes.**
It's _____ francs
_____ centimes.

un one	**deux** two	**trois** three
quatre four	**cinq** five	**six** six
sept seven	**huit** eight	**neuf** nine
dix ten	**onze** eleven	**douze** twelve

treize thirteen	**quatorze** fourteen
quinze fifteen	**seize** sixteen
dix-sept seventeen	**dix-huit** eighteen
dix-neuf nineteen	**vingt** twenty
treize thirty	**quarante** forty
cinquante fifty	**soixante** sixty
soixante-dix seventy	**quatre-vingts** eighty
quatre-vingt-dix ninety	**cent** one hundred
mille one thousand	**dix mille** ten thousand

C'est trop.
It's too much.

Ce n'est pas assez.
It's not enough.

Ça va.
It's all right.

⊘

SIGNET Reference Books (0451)